The Book on Retirement

Are You Ready for the Second Half of Your
Financial Life?

Kevin Houser, CFP®, CES   Gary Plessl, CFP®, CPA

Published by Richter Publishing LLC www.richterpublishing.com

ISBN: 0692356681
ISBN-13: 9780692356685

For Carrie, Ashley, Maddie & Tommy   *For Jake, Livy & Joey*

DEDICATION

Years ago, when we started out in the financial planning business with one of the big firms, we were taught in our early training that we would have difficulty finding a "niche" and becoming experts in that "niche." We were also told that "retired people" was not a "niche" and it was too broad of a category. It did not take us long to realize that those who trained us were 100 percent wrong about the specialized planning needs of retirees – retired people are, in fact, a unique group with a unique set of financial planning needs that differ significantly from the traditional "First Half" approach that many advisors follow. We recognized this early in our careers and have gone to great lengths to understand these needs and find solutions to enable our clients to live their retirement with financial independence.

Because of that, this book is dedicated to a very important group of individuals and families: *our clients*. We are thankful to all of you for patiently listening and considering strategies that in some cases went completely against what you had previously been trained to think. Our hope is that in return, we have enabled you to live a retirement full of financial confidence and independence. Nothing makes us happier than when we hear stories from you of how you are *spending* your money! That is truly what retirement is all about: enjoying the resources you worked so hard to save.

Our relationship with each of you has truly been a two-way street – one that we would call a partnership where both parties benefit. While we hope you have learned something from and benefited from our guidance over the years, we can also tell you that we have learned plenty from you as well. And everything we learned from you, we are sharing with others, just as we share with you what we have learned from others. This virtuous cycle is what continues to make our process more effective in helping clients be better prepared and be able to retire with confidence.

Our hope is that we are able to impress upon our children the wisdom that we have learned in the classroom, in our many years of experience and from you, in the hope that one day they too will be able to enjoy retirement with the same level of independence and confidence that we see in your lives.

Our goal is *to help you* preserve and enjoy the Second Half of your financial life. That is what inspired us to write *The Book on Retirement*.

CONTENTS

Foreword vii

Introduction 1

First Half/Second Half.. 7

First-Half Strategies Can Blow Up Your Retirement 16

IRA/401(K) Ticking Tax Time Bombs 30

Early Retiree and Pre-59 ½ Strategies 41

59 ½ to 70 1/2 : Slow and Steady IRA Distributions Win the Race 52

The Roth IRA: To Convert Or Not To Convert? 61

Reducing Taxes When Your Will "Matures" 73

Do I Need A Trust?.. 88

In Retirement, Cash Flow is King 101

Will I Have Enough?... 110

Foreword

All those years of hard work are finally over. Now you can kick back, relax, travel, spoil your grandkids, play golf and do all the things you've always wanted to do in your golden years, right? Not so fast! That version of the American dream is dead. Today, more and more people are retiring later in life. Sure, some people truly enjoy what they do, so they never quit working. But for most late retirees, it's not a love or obsession for their work that keeps them employed; it's because they don't think they have enough money to retire and simply feel unprepared to make the transition to retirement.

The saddest part about this is that no matter what the stock market is doing or how the economy looks, being forced to stay in the workforce and not retire doesn't have to be an option. For too many people, unfortunately, bad advice and a lack of financial planning is tarnishing those golden years. We're sold on a glut of so-called wisdom that the big houses have rammed down our throats for so many years, and rather than question these tactics and find other ways, we keep doing what we've been doing for years. And how's that working out? Not so well. We have seen countless scenarios where people did a great job in the "First Half" of their financial lives, or the saving and accumulation stage, only to not feel comfortable retiring because they and their "First Half"-focused advisor did not know how to make changes needed for the "Second Half" of their financial lives: the income and distribution phase.

The good news: no matter what you have heard before or what you think you know about planning for retirement, better ways exist. We hope that no matter what your current financial situation, and no matter how much money you have managed to save and put away for retirement, that you use the strategies outlined in this book to help you prepare for retirement.

What's more, our philosophy may be unlike anything you've heard or read about from other financial planners. We believe you should spend your money any way you want in retirement. That's right: spend your money however you want in retirement. After all, you've worked hard all your life, so why not make your golden years memorable by living life to the fullest? This isn't some pipe dream or crazy fantasy. It is very possible to do just this. It comes down to having the correct First-Half financial strategy to properly position you for retirement and then transitioning to the correct Second-Half strategy. The sooner you start, the better prepared you will be. But even if you've made some mistakes, it's never too late to help ensure that tomorrow is better than today.

Throwing money away is probably something we can all agree we would never want to do. But that's exactly what so many people are doing because they haven't been properly educated on how to plan for retirement. With more than 40 years of combined experience in retirement planning, nothing shocks us anymore. We've seen people lose by acting too soon, not acting soon enough, making irrational decisions about their portfolios because of fear and basically giving Uncle Sam money that should have been theirs simply because they were ill-advised or followed the conventional wisdom that most people follow.

In *The Book on Retirement*, we break many of the most common myths and strategies practiced today by other financial planners. You'll learn why taking distributions out of your IRA prior to being forced to by the government is, in many cases, a smart practice even if you don't need the money. You'll learn the real facts about having a trust and even how to withdraw money from an IRA without paying taxes.

To help prepare for an enjoyable retirement, make the decision to start today. While no strategy ensures success or protects against loss, read this book with an open mind. At times, you will read things that go completely against conventional logic – things you have been trained to believe. That's fine. But read the examples, hear us out and ask yourself: has your current strategy really best positioned you for a retirement truly worth living? If the answer is no, it's time to get down to business and start considering the ideas in this book.

We wish you much luck and success in your journey and a prosperous and fulfilling retirement.

- Kevin and Gary

Introduction

Plain and simple: your retirement is in trouble. Those golden days many people have been dreaming about for so long are forever tarnished. Instead of playing golf, spending time with the grandkids and traveling, many retirees are now forced to postpone retirement and stay in the workforce longer. Even when they can finally retire, the life they were expecting to live is anything but enjoyable – and is more about getting by and constantly worrying about whether or not they will run out of money at some point in their retirement.

According to the Employee Benefit Research Institute, the percentage of workers confident about having enough money for a comfortable retirement was at record lows between 2009 and 2013. As of 2014, EBRI numbers indicate that only 18 percent of Americans are very confident they will have enough money to live comfortably in retirement. Additionally, the National Bureau of Economic Research reported in 2012 that 46 percent of American retirees have less than $10,000 in savings at the end of their lives.

These numbers are troubling. It makes you wonder: how do most people ever retire at all? In fact, the late Robert Benmosche, the former chairman of the insurance giant American International Group (AIG), predicted the retirement age would soon increase to somewhere between 70 and 80, to make pensions and medical services more affordable.

Every day, more than 10,000 baby boomers turn 65. That will continue to happen until the year 2019. For most of them, gone are the glory days of taking an early retirement. In fact, forget early: fully 39 percent of workers now plan on retiring after age 65. While there are a number of reasons for this, what most people fail to realize is that with the right financial planning, almost everyone can still retire when they initially planned – provided they do actually plan. It can be done. In fact, one of the most common issues we encounter with new clients is not that they haven't accumulated enough money, but that they simply haven't made the transition from what we call the "accumulation phase" to the "income and distribution phase."

Times have been tougher in recent years as the country fell into what's now known as the "Great Recession," a period when millions of people battled unemployment, started racking up debt and watched their investment portfolios get cut in half. A 2012 study from the Transamerica Center for Retirement Studies says about one third of people who were unemployed or underemployed withdrew from a retirement account despite facing costly penalties, fees and taxes – not to mention, worst of all, delaying their retirement.

The big financial firms are also to blame for improperly preparing Americans for retirement. They've brainwashed us into believing that the only thing each of us needs to do is determine our "magic number" and then save that amount of money before retiring. The problem: that's only half the game! What you do with those assets once you save them provides the real key to a confident and independent retirement.

The problem with saving the pre-determined amount and then thinking you are done is that too many unpredictable variables can affect your retirement. For example, what if you retire at 65 and live to be 100? Will that pre-determined number last 35 years? What if you or your spouse becomes seriously ill and requires very expensive medical care for the rest of your lives, which depletes that predetermined number? What if a market similar to the years 2000-2002 or 2008 happens again during your retirement and your pre-determined number suddenly gets cut in half?

Let's look back at what happened to the stock market between 2000 and 2002. The market crashed largely due to the tech bubble bursting and the September 11, 2001 terrorist attacks.

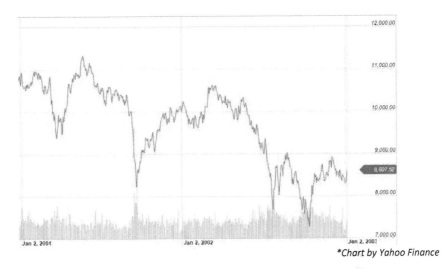

*Chart by Yahoo Finance

People who are prepared for retirement because they have their assets properly positioned (more on this in Chapter 1) are more likely to enjoy a stable income even if the market gets cut in half, and their lifestyle typically does not change much at all. These people will continue doing what they're doing.

Let's say they're living off $100,000 a year, and that income is generated from their pension and Social Security plus 30 percent of their investment assets. That means the other 70 percent of their investment assets are available for additional uses and can be touched without having any impact on their "Steady Eddie" retirement income.

However, it's a different story for the couple who's invested in a 60/40 stock/bond portfolio, and the stock market is down 50 percent. Their overall portfolio is now down 30 percent and they aren't going to feel too good about taking money out at that particular time.

It was a similar situation between June 2007 and March of 2009, when the Dow Jones Industrial Average – which is comprised of 30 stocks that are major factors in their industries and are widely held by individuals and institutional investors – took a nosedive. In less than two years, the Dow went from 13,700 all the way down to 6,700 points.

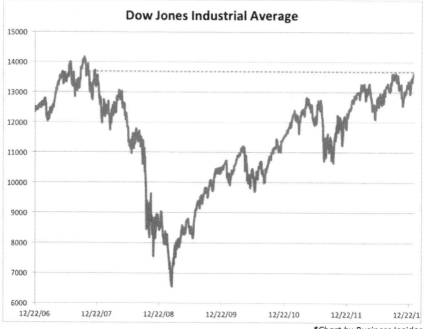

Chart by Business Insider

This was likely due to a combination of factors including the subprime mortgage crisis spreading to government sponsored agencies Fannie Mae and Freddie Mac, requiring a federal government bailout; the bankruptcy announcement of Lehman Brothers; the AIG bailout of $85 billion, which later increased to more than $182.5 billion; and skyrocketing unemployment numbers.

Yet again, for the retiree with his funds properly positioned, the drop in the market wasn't likely an issue.

The bottom line is there are just too many "what if" scenarios. Constantly having to worry about all of these variables and their impact on your pre-determined number is no way to enjoy your retirement. Imagine the couple planning a week-long Caribbean cruise, who suddenly have to downgrade from the cabin with a balcony to an inside stateroom because their pre-determined number is vanishing more quickly than they hoped because the market had a couple of bad months. Sound silly? Situations just like this are playing out every day across America for couples who didn't enter retirement prepared – even for some couples who were responsible about saving during the accumulation phase.

Another common problem we find: couples where only one person, usually the more financially inclined, knows how much money is in retirement savings accounts and how that money is allocated. The problem here: if something unexpectedly happens to that person, the other partner in the relationship is left lost without a clue.

Believe it or not, I (Kevin) was one of those people in a relationship just like this. At the age of 34, I was literally brain dead for 28 minutes during open heart surgery to remove an aneurysm at the root of my heart. Here I was, a CERTIFIED FINANCIAL PLANNER™, and my wife, Carrie, didn't know where the wills and trusts were located, how much insurance we had or what we were invested in. She had left it all up to me.

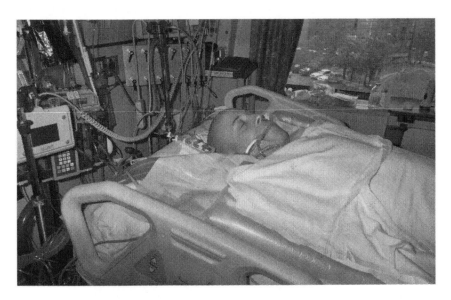

I remember thinking to myself, when I get out of here, not only am I going to make sure my wife is fully prepared and knowledgeable, but I am going to make sure that each and every one of our clients will have the confidence of knowing and feeling prepared – and that both partners in the relationship will know everything that's going on.

Retirement means different things to different people, and as such, the retirement planning process needs to be done on a case-by-case basis. Remember the commercial, "This is not your father's Oldsmobile?" Well, this isn't your father's retirement either. Step No. 1 in our process is getting crystal clear on what you want your retirement to look like. While every situation is different and has its own unique set of variables, the overall structure and strategies involved are essentially the same. Unfortunately, many people, and even many financial planners, are misinformed and full of bad information.

It is our hope that through this book, you will learn how to be prepared for your retirement. That means much more than figuring out an amount of money you must acquire ahead of time. It means knowing how to properly put away enough money until you reach retirement and then making sure you have sufficient cash flow to do the things you want to do in retirement.

Make no mistake about it: doing the things you have always wanted to do in your retirement with financial independence is realistic. The key is proper planning in advance and on an ongoing basis.

Forget everything you've read or heard about retirement. The journey to the Second Half of your financial life starts right now.

Chapter 1

First Half/Second Half

"I don't believe in luck. I believe in preparation."
— Bobby Knight, Hall of Fame basketball coach

When I (Kevin) was just six years old, my "pop-pop," Aloyisious Fitzgerald O'Kennedy, taught me a very important lesson about life. "If you don't know where you are going," he said, "you are never going to get there." Of course at the time, I didn't have a clue what he was talking about. I just stood their nodding my head in agreement.

Ironically, when my grandfather died, the man who gave me that warning about not knowing where you're going didn't know where his own money was going. He didn't plan well for the Second Half of his financial life, and he left my grandmother alone and uncertain about her own retirement and financial future.

Just like my grandfather, a lot of people have the wrong idea about retirement planning. As we've already seen, the statistics are pretty grim for the majority of people entering retirement. Either they're simply not prepared, or they've followed conventional logic that the big firms brainwashed them with. They've received bad advice along the way, and now they are spending their retirement worrying if they will eventually run out of money.

You might even know some of these people. They could be your parents, a close friend or a sibling. Or this might describe your own current situation. Regardless, it's not an enviable position.

In fact, with many of the individuals we talk to, their ultimate questions are, "Will I have enough?" and "Will I have enough to accomplish whatever it is I want to accomplish?"

The good news: it is very possible to do all the things you want during retirement. The bad news: so many people never get to do these things because they simply aren't prepared. Instead of doing all these great things, these people are afraid to spend the money they do have and are stuck worrying about the basics: housing, medical costs, food, transportation, electric bills, etc., when they should be thinking about that special trip they want to take with the grandkids.

If you want your golden years to truly be golden – full of all the things you've always wanted to do with financial independence – the time to prepare is now.

IT STARTS WITH A PLAN

Many people we've met over the years either have, or at one time had, enough money to retire with the lifestyle they wanted. The problem: they never put a plan in place to carry out those retirement dreams with financial confidence. Every good venture starts out with a solid plan. Retirement is no different. A well thought out plan for your retirement is the key to enjoying the Second Half of your life. And the earlier you develop this plan, the better.

Do you really want to go through your retirement looking at your financial statements, worrying about every penny and trying to determine if you have the ability to do the things you've always wanted to do? That's no way to enjoy what should be one of the greatest times of your life.

So many retirees are trapped watching the stock market on a day-to-day basis. When the market's up, they are full of excitement, and they're planning that dream vacation or buying a new car – doing all the things they have been dreaming about. When the market's down, it's a very different story. These same people act very differently. They are living in a world of constant fear and worry.

The Second Half should be a time to enjoy your life. Money should not be one of your worries if you're prepared and have received the right financial advice along the way. Most of the people we meet are scared. Many of them watched in horror as their holdings evaporated between 2000 and 2002. Then, just as they were getting back on their feet, it happened again in 2008. Not only are they worried that they won't be able to do great things for their kids and grandkids in retirement. They're not even sure they will be able to do all the great things they wanted to do for themselves.

Nowadays, many people want to take everything they have and protect it. In a sense, they have become money hoarders. We once had a client tell us she keeps so much money under her pillow that her neck hurt. These kinds of people just want to put all their money in a lockbox and leave it there. They've worked their entire life and saved this big bucket of money, and now they are afraid to lose it – or in many cases even use it.

That might sound extreme. But considering all the horror stories of people losing everything – and the lack of good information about how to avoid falling victim to that – can we really blame these people? Until they have a solid financial plan, where all their money is laid out in front of them, they have no idea how much they can take out and enjoy. It has a psychological as well as a financial impact on them.

As we've said, retirement is about enjoying your life to the fullest without having to worry about money. When you're prepared for retirement, you can spend and enjoy your money however you want.

THE THREE BUCKETS OF CASH FLOW

When we talk about having enough money for retirement, we like to use the "three buckets of cash flow," which clearly lay out where all your money is at any given moment. The advantage to using a roadmap like this is that there's plenty of money to live off of right now so you can actually enjoy your retirement, while you also have plenty put away for emergencies and other unexpected events. Meanwhile, parts of that lump sum continue to grow, enabling you to leave it to your children, grandchildren or whomever else you decide.

Bucket No. 1: Cash and liquidity
This is our ready-access cash, the money that enables us to walk into a bank and walk out with greenbacks in hand.

Bucket No. 2: First-Half investments
This is our next line of defense. These assets are positioned for growth and income but serve as a back-up in case you need to access money right away. For example: a down payment on a car or a new roof on your home. These assets are typically accessible within three business days with no penalties.

Bucket No. 3: Second-Half investments
These assets are specifically positioned to provide you with 100 percent of your retirement income when combined with any other income you are receiving on a monthly basis (i.e., pension, Social Security, etc.)

Every bucket is there to accomplish a goal. If someone is trying to accomplish another specific goal, like assisting grandkids with education or providing cash flow to maintain the family house at the beach, then we might add a fourth bucket with assets to pursue that goal.

We like to break down the retirement process into two categories: the First Half of your financial life and the Second Half of your financial life. The logic behind this concept is simple: with the right financial planning in the First Half, you can live the life you want and do the things you have always dreamed about doing in the Second Half.

There's no catch to the formula, and we're not going to tell you that you need to put away a ridiculous amount of money and suffer through the First Half of your financial life. In fact, the opposite is true. To deprive you of having fun or spending any money in the First Half of your financial life is not the goal; you should enjoy that time, too, and have plenty of money to not only do the things you want to do but also to pay the bills and everyday living expenses that are a part of life.

It is, however, necessary during the First Half to start thinking about the Second Half – and to start putting away money for retirement as early as possible.

THE FIRST HALF

The First Half of your financial life is the accumulation phase. It starts the moment you enter the workforce and ends when you retire. The main goal for everyone during this time, as it relates to retirement, is to accumulate as much money as possible into an IRA, 401(k) account or other savings for retirement. If your employer is willing to match up to a certain percentage of your contributions, that's an added bonus; after all, it's as if someone just opened their wallet and handed you some extra cash.

During the First Half, time is on your side. If the market takes a dip, it's not devastating because you're a long-term investor with plenty of time to recover. You can afford to weather the storm and ride the ups and downs of the roller coaster.

Vanguard Group co-founder John "Jack" Bogle told CNBC he suspected stocks would grow annually "something like 5 percent over the next decade – 5 percent a year, some years way ahead of that, some years down, some years behind that." The interviewers didn't press him to be more precise about which specific years would be up and which would be down. Had they done so, he probably would have replied that he didn't know the answer. *And the answer wouldn't matter anyway for long-term investors during the accumulation phase, or the First Half, of their financial lives.*

First-Half financial planning tools and investment models force investors into a handful of cookie-cutter models in an attempt to invest their assets to maximize the growth during this accumulation phase. Investments tend to be widespread, focusing on both conservative and more aggressive allocations.

Unfortunately, as baby boomers get closer to age 65, many of them fail to realize that the strategies that help them accumulate assets during the First Half of their financial lives may not work as effectively during the Second Half of their financial lives.

THE SECOND HALF

The big day is finally here. There's a big cake with your name on it in the break room, and someone from the executive office presents you with a plaque recognizing your milestone. You walk out of that building for the last time, eager to start your retirement and wondering what you'll do first.

Now the game changes. In Second-Half financial planning, there are no "model portfolios" or "cookie-cutter asset allocation portfolios" to follow. Even though we might use a handful of tools that we like and use for other clients, we use different percentages for each client to best position that client's dollars to solve for cash flow. Every dollar that you have today is positioned to pursue a goal. In retirement, cash flow is king!

We position your investments first and foremost to solve for your specific cash flow needs. How much income we need to generate from your portfolio will dictate how much we allocate to the different buckets. If we could get to a spot where 30 to 50 percent of your assets are (combined with Social Security and pension income) generating 100 percent of your retirement income, that leaves 50 to 70 percent of your assets that are just there as an additional cushion that's readily accessible for any lump-sum needs that might arise during retirement.

The Second Half of your financial life is about the Three Ps: protecting, preserving and passing along your assets.

If the market all of a sudden gets cut in half a year after retirement, you don't want it to impact your lifestyle. Running out of money or coming close to running out of money should never come into play. In fact, we are probably two of the few financial planners who actually encourage our clients to spend their money in retirement. Yes, you heard that right: we encourage our clients to spend their money in retirement because that's what it's there for – and because there is enough of it to do just that.

The Second-Half decisions are:

- What happens to my retirement income stream if the stock market takes a dip?

- How do I get all of that money from the First Half out of those retirement accounts without paying too much income tax?

- What happens to all of that money if something happens to me?

- How can I make sure my assets stay in my family and go to whom I want them to go to?

EXPECT THE UNEXPECTED

Like everything else in life, retirement carries no guarantees. The market could drop significantly, or you or your spouse could die unexpectedly. In the Second Half of your financial life, it's important to know that no matter what happens, you're going to be okay financially. Having that confidence is the key when the unexpected happens.

Mike and Connie had been clients of ours for many years. From the very first meeting, Mike always stressed how he wanted to one day retire and play tennis every single day of retirement. Thankfully, with their diligence and our guidance, they prepared so well for their retirement that they were actually able to retire a few years early. We met with them twice a year prior to their retirement, as we do with all of our clients.

When Mike and Connie finally retired, they came into our office with big smiles on their faces and told us they found their dream home in a gated country club community near the Pacific Ocean in California and wanted to make sure that a big purchase like this wouldn't affect their retirement. We looked at each of their buckets and assured them they had plenty of money to go ahead with the purchase. Mike was like a kid in a candy shop and was looking forward to playing tennis every day and taking his grandchildren to the beach.

A week after they moved, Mike called us to tell us he had just been diagnosed with cancer and wanted to make sure that if anything happened to him, Connie would be financially taken care of for the rest of her life. One year to the day after Mike's diagnosis, he lost a courageous battle against cancer and died.

We flew to California, on our own dime, to meet face to face with Connie. We went over every aspect of the Second-Half financial plan that we had created with Mike and Connie during the past few years. By having a financial plan in place and having enough money allocated in each of their buckets, Connie has been able to continue her retirement without worrying about having enough money. The loss of her husband was devastating, but thankfully she didn't have to worry about her financial situation because, as we like to say, cash flow doesn't lie. And thanks to years of solid financial planning for the Second Half of life, the cash flow was indeed there for Connie.

The story of Mike and Connie is a sad one. And unfortunately, it's one that happens all too often. While no one can predict exactly when it will be their time, having a solid financial plan in place – one of which both partners are aware – will provide confidence for both of you as you live out your retirement.

Chapter 1 Dividends

1. A well-thought-out plan, begun early, is the key to a financially healthy retirement.

2. The First Half of your financial life is about accumulating wealth.

3. The Second Half of your financial life is more about protecting, preserving and passing along that wealth.

4. The key to a successful retirement is transitioning from a First-Half strategy to a Second-Half strategy.

Chapter 2

First-Half Strategies Can Blow Up Your Retirement

"Things change. And friends leave. Life doesn't stop for anybody."
— Stephen Chbosky, The Perks of Being a Wallflower

THE ONLY CONSTANT IS CHANGE

Based on more than 40 years of combined experience in the business, the one thing we've learned you can always expect is change. Everything will change. The world around us will change. Our friends will change. Your tastes will change: one day you'll wake up and realize something you once couldn't stand the thought of, you suddenly enjoy. Specific to retirement, the tax laws will change; the markets will change on a daily basis; and the price of what you're doing for your lifestyle is going to change.

So the only constant, as the paradoxical saying goes, is change. And although everything is always changing, one thing should never change: having the ability to enjoy your retirement. Regardless how the economy is changing, what the market is doing or anything else, if you're truly going be able to do the things you want to do in the Second Half, you must be prepared, and that's why having a solid Second-Half financial strategy is crucial.

Look how much has changed during the past 15 years of the stock market. There was the rise and fall of the dot-com era. New technology companies took off from 1997-2000 and then came crashing down between 2000 and 2001. Many that seemed so promising failed completely. Others like Amazon.com managed to hang on and proved just how much the market can change. Its share price went from $107 to $7 but a decade later exceeded $200.

The Dow Jones Industrial Average has changed significantly too. In September and October of 2012, the Dow broke 13,500 on its way to more than 17,000 by the middle of 2014. In early 2009, the picture wasn't nearly as pretty: the Dow had sunk below 7,000.

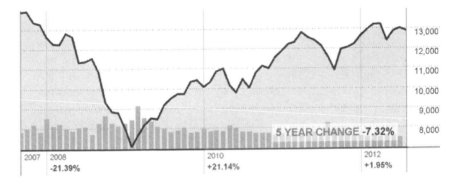

Chart by CNN Money

Even with such drastic ups and downs in such little time, those who had a plan using Second-Half strategies were generally able to continue enjoying their retirement – and were still doing the things they wanted to do.

The biggest changes often take place as people go through retirement. At first, you might have big dreams of traveling the globe or playing golf as much as you want. But then along comes the first grandchild, and now all you want to do is stay home and watch him or her grow up. Where you want to spend your money will also probably change: now you want to spoil your grandchild with clothing, toys and other items.

Also changing in the big picture is where or to whom your money will go once you leave this world. You'll probably want to allocate a certain amount of money to your grandchildren or contribute to an education fund for them.

With so many changes constantly taking place, it's imperative to use Second-Half financial strategies in retirement. We have talked to so many retirees trying to use a First-Half approach while living in the Second Half. These people have ended up living their retirement constantly worrying about whether they will have enough to accomplish whatever it is they want to accomplish.

THE BIGGEST CHANGE OF ALL: THE DEATH OF A SPOUSE

One thing most couples don't think much about when they retire is what happens when the husband or wife dies – and what the income impact on the surviving spouse will be. Some very significant changes take place that most people are unaware of or simply choose to ignore.

When we meet with people and ask about the survivor benefits of their pensions, the answer we usually hear is, "I don't know." When you die, does your spouse get 100 percent of your pension, 50 percent of your pension or nothing at all? This is very crucial information to be aware of, because a large chunk of cash flow might disappear for the surviving spouse.

The other thing people don't realize is just how much of your retirement cash flow depends on Social Security – and what happens when a spouse dies. The survivor is going to get the higher of the two Social Security checks. If the husband has the higher of the two and he passes away, the wife will lose her Social Security benefits and start receiving only his.

An example of just how critical survivor benefits are:

Let's say your spouse passes away. His pension was $34,000 annually, and he has a 50 percent survivor benefit. Now the surviving spouse is only receiving $17,000 a year from that pension. Social Security was $20,000 a year for him and $10,000 a year for her. So instead of receiving $30,000 a year in Social Security, the surviving spouse will only receive $20,000. That's another $10,000 a year off the table. In this scenario, the surviving spouse is down $27,000 a year of cash flow that was coming in. What's going to replace it?

If there's nothing set up to make up for the loss, now you have a surviving spouse who just lost her husband and is somehow going to have to start generating some additional income from her portfolio, which will leave her making capricious decisions on the fly. Life is going to be very different without your spouse, and it's going to bring about major changes in your life. But your finances are something that can be controlled, and your income doesn't need to change if you're properly prepared ahead of time. Remember the story of Mike and Connie in Chapter 1? One year into retirement Mike passed away, and although this was obviously a terrible life-changing event for Connie, at least she had financial independence, because they were prepared.

On top of that, timing is everything. No one can control when they are going to make their exit from this world. If we could control it, we would all want to do it when the market is up.

If you happen to die at the wrong time, when the market is down, this has a significant impact on the survivor.

This goes back to the point that it's imperative for both partners in the relationship to be involved in retirement planning. You're going to have enough challenges to deal with when your spouse dies. Finances shouldn't be one of them. If you're the spouse in the relationship who just lets the other person make all the important decisions and you don't understand your will, don't know where your money is invested or don't know what happens to your income once your spouse dies, now is the time to make sure there is a Second-Half plan in place before it's too late.

BIG MARKET DROP AT THE WRONG TIME

Unfortunately, another big problem, whether you plan on working during retirement or not, is that many people are still following those First-Half strategies during the Second Half. These very same strategies, which once made perfect sense, can easily backfire during retirement. Perhaps one of the biggest and most necessary changes that comes with retirement is changing from First-Half financial strategies to Second-Half financial strategies – or put another way, shifting from "savings and accumulation mode" to "preservation and protection mode." Without this critical change in how you manage your money, you're potentially headed for financial disaster.

We've already established the differences between First-Half strategies and Second-Half strategies. The First Half of your financial life is the accumulation phase; Second-Half financial strategies focus on protecting, preserving and passing along your assets as well as planning out income and distribution strategies and – most importantly – not having to spend your retirement worrying about what the market is doing.

Despite all these changes constantly taking place, most people aren't prepared for retirement. According to a 2012 report from the Transamerica Retirement Survey, the majority of workers in their 50s and 60s plan to work after they retire, with 43 percent reporting that they plan to work part time and 11 percent reporting that they plan to work full time. Only 19 percent of retirees do not plan on working at all in retirement, while 27 percent are unsure what their plans are.

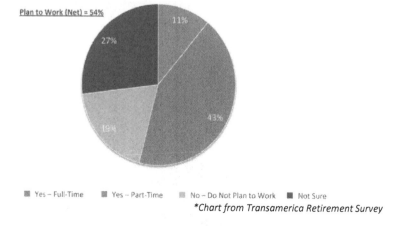

Plan to Work (Net) = 54%

■ Yes – Full-Time   ■ Yes – Part-Time   ■ No – Do Not Plan to Work   ■ Not Sure

Chart from Transamerica Retirement Survey

That means more than half – fully 54 percent – of the population plans on working in some capacity after they officially retire. It's one thing if you work to avoid boredom or to dabble in a field that you always found interesting but never had the time to explore. However, working after retirement should never be about supplementing your post-retirement income. That just means you weren't prepared. We often tell our clients that we have them in a plan where they are working because they *want* to work, not because they *have* to work.

Before people retire, they typically follow a strategy where they have a certain comfort level with risk. They have a certain percentage of their portfolio invested in stocks and a certain percentage in bonds or other fixed-income investments. For the purposes of discussion, let's say it's 60 percent in stocks and 40 percent in bonds or other fixed-income investments.

Over time, those investments will go up and down. But over a long period of time the investments will do okay. When those dips occur, it's not a big deal because you're a long-term investor and are not looking to use that money right away. (If anything, the dips give you a chance to accumulate more shares at a discount.)

Once you retire, let's say you've accumulated $500,000 and are drawing 5 percent as an income stream. That's $25,000 annually with the hope the market is going to rise enough to replenish that 5 percent. What happens when you wake up one morning and the market crashes, and your $500,000 all of a sudden becomes $250,000, and you're still drawing $25,000 a year from it? Now you're not drawing 5 percent. You're drawing 10 percent of your portfolio, and the problem can snowball quickly. We call this "circling the drain."

The problem in this particular situation is not only financial but also psychological. When you were working, you had stuff to do, things to keep you busy and occupy your time. Now with more free time on your hands, you sit in front of the TV and watch the market all day. With more free time to watch and worry as your money disappears because the market is tanking, you become nervous and decide to step in and take what you believe to be corrective action.

Acting out of fear, you take the money out of an account that is already depressed, and invest it in an ultra-conservative portfolio, and as a result you miss the market bounce-back. You have just made an emotional – not a financial – decision. We met Jack, a retired engineer, back in 2009. When his portfolio was dropping in 2008, he made this very emotional decision and moved his entire portfolio to cash and subsequently missed one of the greatest market recoveries in history. You're likely going to have that plus 20 percent year in retirement, but you'll also likely have that minus 20 percent year at some point. When you let fear get in the way, you end up adding insult to injury.

On top of that, keep in mind that at "the big houses" the brokers get paid based on how much you buy and sell, not how well you do. When you sell your assets, you pay a transaction fee. What happens once you sell? The broker will typically talk you into buying another position, yielding yet another commission and/or transaction fee. Selling a stock to buy a bond is a transaction cost. So now, you're jumping from a fire into a pot that's boiling. You're paying penalties to get out of something you perceive as dangerous, when if you generally should just sit tight, the market would eventually recover. You've lost money and the ability to do the things you want to do because the market is temporarily not cooperating.

This is yet another example of how following First-Half financial planning strategies in the Second Half can blow up your retirement. Second-Half strategies are designed for income and distribution as well as preservation. Following the bucket approach, mentioned earlier, has your money allocated in different buckets where they are specifically invested to pursue some goal or some purpose. This strategy has helped our clients continue living their retirement without any adjustments to their cash flow even when the market does not cooperate.

We have also talked to many individuals who believe the best approach once they retire is to move all of their money to CDs and other fixed-income portfolios. The problem here is obvious: this approach provides no preparation against inflation. If you retire at age 65 and have a 25-year retirement, there is a pretty good chance that inflation will drastically reduce the purchasing power of your CDs. In turn, as your expenses increase you will simply draw down those assets and start "circling the drain." Here again, we have also found a psychological component to how these individuals are living their retirement, with a constant fear of running out of money and being afraid to spend any of their assets in retirement. Our clients have found that the Second-Half strategies that we have put in place for them help them to live their retirement and spend their money – which is exactly the reason you saved it all those years.

CONVENTIONAL LOGIC FOR IRA DISTRIBUTION IS ALL WRONG

Most people follow what we call "conventional logic" when it comes to taking distributions from their IRA accounts. In fact, we would go as far as saying almost every person we have ever spoken to follows conventional logic with IRA distributions. Conventional logic says to let your IRA money grow tax deferred as long as you possibly can. That's not bad advice. But it's not always the best advice.

The potential problem begins when you turn 70 ½. That's when the government requires you to start withdrawing money from your traditional tax-deferred IRA accounts, whether you really need it or not, in the form of required minimum distributions (RMDs). The older you are, the larger a percentage of your IRA account you have to take out, which can push you into a higher tax bracket.

What we have found with many of our clients, by doing some additional analysis, is that they actually end up paying less in taxes by taking some money out of their IRA accounts before they turn 70 ½ even if they don't need the money to live. (Everyone's tax situation will vary, and it is important to speak to a qualified tax advisor prior to making any withdrawal decisions. It is also important to note that withdrawals prior to the age of 59 ½ can result in penalties.)

An optimally effective IRA distribution strategy is designed to get the money out of your IRA at the lowest possible tax rate. The important thing is to constantly review your tax situation looking for those opportunities. This needs to be a proactive strategy because once those opportunities are missed, there is no way to go back.

In Chapter 5, we'll go into more detail about this and provide more specific examples of why conventional logic doesn't always work. In many of the plans we establish, we're taking distributions from IRA accounts prior to people reaching age 70 ½ because tax wise it typically makes sense to do it.

Financial advisors who come from the school of "First-Half strategies are the way to go forever" – they won't characterize it quite that way, but that's what they are advocating – rarely are able to look beyond this conventional logic. Since Gary is not just a CFP® but also a CPA, we are able to look at the tax benefits of going against this conventional logic. The potential tax savings mean the contrarian strategy – earlier-than-necessary withdrawals – is a tool that should not be overlooked.

In the First Half, most people aren't paying too much attention to their tax returns. Their income is what it is, their deductions are what they are and – if they are diligent – they're putting as much money as they possibly can into a retirement account. When you retire, it's a completely different game. You no longer have the steady salary. Now you have much more flexibility in controlling what your income is going to be each year by managing your IRA distributions. By properly planning this with an advisor who is knowledgeable about taxes (someone who is a CPA) and can give you tax advice, you can make sure you're doing things as tax efficiently as possible.

Taxes are a much bigger piece of the puzzle than most people realize. People will often say they have a CPA who does their taxes. But in most cases CPAs have so much on their plates, especially in February, March and April, that they're not doing tax planning because they are just trying to get through the day. They are too busy crunching the numbers and getting the returns done. The other problem: most of the time, the CPA and financial advisor are never talking. The CPA doesn't know what the financial advisor is doing, and the financial advisor doesn't know what the CPA is doing. To take it a step further, there's usually a multilateral disconnect between the insurance agent, the CPA, the estate attorney and the financial advisor. Often times, not only do these different professionals not talk, but they assume the other areas of a plan are already handled. We prefer to "quarterback" the advisory team and make sure the taxes, legal, insurance and investments are all working together toward the same goal: your care-free retirement. Having this type of a relationship is critical to the success of a comprehensive Second-Half plan.

LONGEVITY PLANNING

In 2010, the average life expectancy in the United States was 78.2 years. How long will you or your spouse live? There's obviously no way to predict that. But the answer – financially speaking, anyway! – can be surprisingly unimportant if you follow Second-Half financial strategies. If you do, you will have a much higher degree of confidence that you will 1) have the money to do the things you want to do, 2) pay for medical care as you age and 3) have enough left over to leave a legacy for your children, grandchildren and great-grandchildren – all regardless of how long you live.

We have met with so many people living the Second Half who are just taking from that one big bucket – their portfolio. So they end up stuck with the mindset of "I need to make it last" and are literally afraid to spend their money.

The key: the market doesn't need to go down and stay down to ruin your retirement. All that needs to happen is a bear market *at the wrong time*. If that happens, the sustainability of your retirement income can take a significant hit.

The "sequence of returns" on the next page helps to explain how a bad market at the wrong time can drastically change your retirement. The sequence of returns might not have much of an impact on the portfolio of a long-term investor who is *accumulating assets* for retirement. But *during* retirement, the sequence of returns can have a dramatic impact on a portfolio's ability to last.

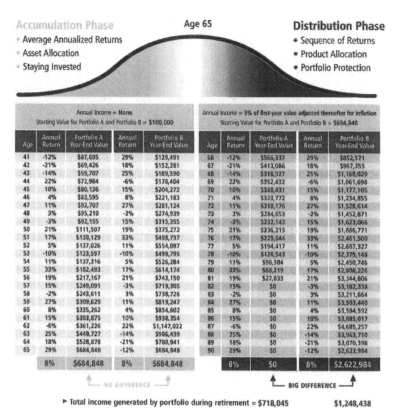

Accumulation Phase
- Average Annualized Returns
- Asset Allocation
- Staying Invested

Age 65

Distribution Phase
- Sequence of Returns
- Product Allocation
- Portfolio Protection

Annual Income = None
Starting Value for Portfolio A and Portfolio B = $100,000

Age	Annual Return	Portfolio A Year-End Value	Annual Return	Portfolio B Year-End Value
41	-12%	$87,695	29%	$129,491
42	-21%	$69,426	18%	$152,281
43	-14%	$59,707	25%	$189,590
44	22%	$72,984	-6%	$178,404
45	10%	$80,136	15%	$204,272
46	4%	$83,595	8%	$221,183
47	11%	$92,707	27%	$281,124
48	3%	$95,210	-2%	$274,939
49	-3%	$92,155	15%	$315,355
50	21%	$111,507	19%	$375,272
51	17%	$130,129	33%	$498,737
52	5%	$137,026	11%	$554,097
53	-10%	$123,597	-10%	$499,795
54	11%	$137,316	5%	$526,284
55	33%	$182,493	17%	$614,174
56	19%	$217,167	21%	$743,150
57	15%	$249,091	-3%	$719,305
58	-2%	$243,611	3%	$738,726
59	27%	$309,629	11%	$819,247
60	8%	$335,262	4%	$854,602
61	15%	$383,875	10%	$938,354
62	-6%	$361,226	22%	$1,147,022
63	25%	$449,727	-14%	$986,439
64	18%	$528,878	-21%	$780,941
65	29%	$684,848	-12%	$684,848
	8%	**$684,848**	**8%**	**$684,848**

Annual Income = 5% of first-year value adjusted thereafter for inflation
Starting Value for Portfolio A and Portfolio B = $684,848

Age	Annual Return	Portfolio A Year-End Value	Annual Return	Portfolio B Year-End Value
66	-12%	$566,337	29%	$852,571
67	-21%	$413,086	18%	$967,355
68	-14%	$316,927	25%	$1,168,029
69	22%	$352,432	-6%	$1,061,698
70	10%	$348,431	15%	$1,177,105
71	4%	$323,772	8%	$1,234,855
72	11%	$318,176	27%	$1,528,614
73	3%	$284,653	-2%	$1,452,871
74	-3%	$232,143	15%	$1,623,066
75	21%	$236,215	19%	$1,886,771
76	17%	$229,644	33%	$2,461,500
77	5%	$194,417	11%	$2,687,327
78	-10%	$126,543	-10%	$2,375,148
79	11%	$90,304	5%	$2,450,746
80	33%	$68,219	17%	$2,808,226
81	19%	$27,833	21%	$3,344,606
82	15%	$0	-3%	$3,182,338
83	-2%	$0	3%	$3,211,664
84	27%	$0	11%	$3,593,440
85	8%	$0	4%	$3,594,592
86	15%	$0	10%	$3,885,017
87	-6%	$0	22%	$4,685,257
88	25%	$0	-14%	$3,963,710
89	18%	$0	-21%	$3,070,398
90	29%	$0	-12%	$2,622,984
	8%	**$0**	**8%**	**$2,622,984**

⌐ NO DIFFERENCE ⌐   ⌐ BIG DIFFERENCE ⌐

► Total income generated by portfolio during retirement = $718,045 $1,248,438

The sequence of returns has an average compounded annualized return of 8% over 25 years and year-to-year volatility that is consistent with a portfolio predominantly comprised of stocks. Annual returns have been rounded to the nearest whole number. The accumulation portfolios assume a starting value of $100,000 at age 40 and no annual withdrawals. The distribution portfolios assume a starting value of either $100,000 or $684,848 at age 65 as well as a 5% first-year withdrawal thereafter adjusted for 3% inflation annually. Except where noted, the average annualized return for the 25-year period is 8%. Source: Standard & Poor's.

The chart shows us the actual rate of return of the Standard & Poor's 500 Index over 25 years. (The S&P 500 is a capitalization-weighted index of 500 stocks designed to measure performance of the broad domestic economy through changes in the aggregate market value of 500 stocks representing all major industries.) Investor A began with an investment of $100,000. Investor B also began with the same $100,000 investment, but the annual S&P 500 returns are flipped completely upside down: the last year's return is now the first. On the left, during the accumulation phase, both investors are working and not touching their savings; on the right, during the distribution phase, they are both withdrawing 5 percent annually. On both sides of the chart, despite the many market swings, both investors – because all the same annual returns are present, just in different orders – average the same 8 percent returns annually during the 25-year-period.

And guess what? When both investors were working (on the left), even though everything happened in a completely different order, and even though at some points (such as when both investors were in their 50s) Investor B had more than triple the nest egg of Investor A, at the end of the 25-year period, they both ended up with exactly the same amount of money. When you're working, you have time on your side. You aren't concerned about the ups and downs of the market. You can see clearly that during the accumulation phase on the left, when no distributions are taken, both investor A and B end up with exactly the same amount of money at the end of the 25-year span, despite the fact that their annual returns were achieved in reverse order.

In retirement, however, it is a much different story. During the Second Half of your financial life, having an income and distribution strategy in place becomes exceptionally critical. As you can see, during the distribution phase on the right, if Investor A and Investor B withdraw 5 percent of the initial amount out of their portfolio every year, Investor A runs out of money by age 82 while Investor B still has $2.6 million at age 90. How is this possible when they both achieved the same average annual return over the 25 year span and they both started out with exactly the same amount of money? The answer is simple: a bad market at the wrong time for Investor A. Investor A had a down market for the first 3 years of retirement. As you can see, Investor A "circled the drain" completely and ran out of money at age 82.

The lesson from the chart: it's okay to have a bear market during retirement, but it's not okay to have a bear market during the early years of retirement if you don't have a Second-Half plan. Almost everybody knows the market will have bad years. But almost nobody knows when these bad years will occur. That's a problem for someone who is following First-Half strategies during life's Second Half, whereas it matters surprisingly little for someone following appropriate Second-Half strategies during the Second Half. (This is a hypothetical example and is not representative of any specific situation. Your results will vary. The hypothetical rates of return used do not reflect the deduction of fees and charges inherent to investing. Indices cannot be invested into directly. Index performance is not indicative of the performance of any investment. Past performance is no guarantee of future results.)

TRUST AND COMMUNICATION

As in any good partnership, the keys to success are trust and communication. Without them, you're likely destined for failure. Even the most skilled financial advisor in the world is going to have a difficult time staying in business if he doesn't build trust and establish a strong rapport with his clients.

Trust and communication with your financial advisor are critical to being prepared for the Second Half of your financial life. Many of the people we now work with seem to have had an issue in one of these areas with their previous advisors. In some cases, these lapses – which might not really seem like financial issues – almost destroyed some portfolios.

It's not that their advisors were intentionally trying not to prepare clients for the Second Half. It's that they were probably still stuck on the old mantra that stocks are going to outperform bonds, and you're a long-term investor. The problem is, when you're 65 years old, you're not such a long-term investor anymore.

If you do consider yourself a long-term investor at age 65, it's probably not so much about you but about your kids. In that case, let's get your portfolio set up so that it's positioned properly for them.

Your financial advisor needs to look at you as an individual, or at you and your spouse as a couple, and make sure 1) first and foremost there is a proper income and distribution strategy in place and 2) your assets are positioned with Second-Half strategies to protect, preserve and pass those assets along.

Chapter 2 Dividends

1. A Second-Half financial strategy must accommodate the one constant in life: change.

2. Having *both* spouses involved in the Second-Half plan is imperative.

3. Following First-Half strategies in the Second Half can lead to financial disaster.

4. How you manage your IRA distributions can impact what you pay in taxes.

5. Having a Second Half plan in place can make a bear market... well... "bear"able even in retirement.

Chapter 3

IRA/401(k) Ticking Tax Time Bombs

"I am proud to be paying taxes in the United States. The only thing is, I could be just as proud for half the money."

— Arthur Godfrey, TV broadcaster

We have all heard the saying that only two things in life – death and taxes – are certain. But most investors don't realize the significant tax hit waiting for them once they retire. And then once they do feel the impact of the tax bite, they think that's the way it has to be. Many people don't realize they can take a few simple steps to potentially minimize their tax burden during retirement.

Most people would agree that retirement accounts such as IRAs or 401(k)s are great ways to save money for retirement. The government strongly encourages us to contribute to these accounts by offering us a tax deduction for the money we put in and then allowing tax-deferred growth on our investments. This is a great deal! But the catch: at some point, that money needs to come out. And the taxes need to be paid.

Think about it this way: if you have $1 million in an IRA, you don't really have $1 million, because to actually use that money,

you need to take it out of the IRA and pay the taxes on all the money that has never been taxed.

That is why we refer to IRAs and 401(k)s as "ticking tax time bombs." It's only a matter of time until that money will come out, and all those taxes will need to be paid.

The trick to diffusing the ticking tax time bomb inside your IRA is to have an income and distribution strategy designed to not only meet your cash flow needs, but also to minimize the taxes you will have to pay on all that money sitting in your IRA or 401(k).

FINANCIAL LIFE PHASES

Your age plays a significant role in your retirement cash flow as well as the taxes you pay. You need to focus on several key "financial life phases:"

Pre 59 ½: Prior to reaching age 59 ½, most people are typically still in the pre-retirement savings and accumulation mode. Most people would agree that while you are working, a good strategy is to sock away as much money as possible into IRA and 401(k) accounts, taking advantage of the tax deductions and letting that money continue to grow tax deferred. It's a simple strategy that makes complete sense, because it reduces your income tax bill while you are working and are in a higher tax bracket than the one in which you will probably be when you retire.

Of course, it's a different story if you want to retire early and get money out of those retirement accounts before you turn 59 ½. In that case, you will have to jump through some hurdles to avoid getting hit with a 10 percent premature distribution penalty from the IRS. We will touch on this in more detail in Chapter 4.

59 ½ to 70 ½: During this phase, the government gives you a choice: take distributions from your retirement accounts without any penalty, although you would still need to pay the taxes on the distributions, or leave the money in your retirement account for continued tax-deferred growth opportunities. Most people in this phase follow conventional logic, which says if you do not need the money to live, then your best strategy is to leave the money in the retirement accounts to continue to grow tax deferred as long as possible. Why – this thinking goes – would you ever want to pay taxes on distributions you don't even need? While this seems logical, we have found many situations where this conventional logic may not reduce your total taxes. We will discuss this in more detail in Chapter 5.

70 ½ and older: By this time the government says, "enough is enough;" you've had that money in your retirement accounts long enough, and it's time to start taking it out in the form of "required minimum distributions" (RMDs). The IRS uses a formula based on your IRA account values as of Dec. 31 and a pre-determined life expectancy to calculate your RMD amount. The RMD amount will vary each year. And this is when the conventional logic followed during the 59 ½-to-70 ½ time frame can really backfire on you. We have seen countless situations where the amount people are now forced to withdraw pushes them into a higher tax bracket.

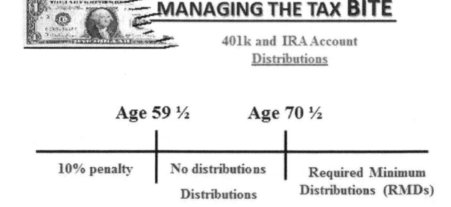

MANAGING THE TAX BITE

401k and IRA Account
Distributions

Age 59 ½   Age 70 ½

10% penalty | No distributions | Required Minimum
            | Distributions | Distributions (RMDs)

SQUEEZING THE BRACKETS

Following that conventional logic of putting away as much money as you can and letting it grow tax deferred isn't the worst advice – after all, anyone who is diligently saving for retirement is doing more than most Americans. But it can have its drawbacks, too. Most people we speak with delay taking any money out of their retirement accounts until they are forced to at 70 ½ through RMDs. The problem: now the amount they must take out at age 70 ½ is often much more than they need to live. This typically throws them into a higher tax bracket. Since we plan for both the taxes and the financial planning for many of our clients, what we have found, with some additional analysis, is that taking some money out of your IRA accounts prior to age 70 ½, even when you don't need to, can help lower your overall tax bill throughout your retirement.

Again, IRAs and 401(k) accounts are great: you can put money away and get a tax deduction, and then the money grows tax deferred. But you know the saying, "What goes up must come down?" Well the corollary to that with retirement planning is, "What goes in must come out." And when it comes out, it's time to pay the taxes. The trick is to balance an income and distribution strategy designed to not only give you the income you need to enjoy your lifestyle, but also to minimize the taxes you pay as the money comes out of your retirement account.

As we mentioned earlier, some of the money in your IRA and 401(k), in a sense, is not real money. That's because when you take the money out of the accounts, you are forced to pay the taxes on this money, which has never been taxed. There is no way to avoid this. Depending on how and when the money comes out of the account, the tax hit could be as much as 39.6 percent. That is quite a significant reduction.

When we set up financial plans for our clients, one of our main strategies is to get the money out of their retirement accounts at the lowest possible tax rate. We call this "squeezing the brackets." On the surface, taking money you don't yet need out of your retirement accounts prior to 70 ½ might not seem logical. But in the long run, doing so can provide you and your family with potentially substantial tax savings. This is where going against conventional logic can really help you.

Let's look at the hypothetical example of a married couple with a pension of $30,000 a year and a combined Social Security income of $30,000 a year. In this case, tax rules dictate that about 50 percent of that Social Security income will be taxable. Let's also say the couple has an additional $10,000 of interest and dividend income. Add it all up, and their adjusted gross income – adjusting for the portion of Social Security income that's not taxable – is $55,350. They are entitled to their standard deduction, which in this case is $12,200, and they each get a personal exemption of $3,900, or $7,800 for the two of them. Their taxable income is $35,350.

For a married couple filing jointly, they are well within the 15 percent tax bracket, which goes all the way up to $72,500[1]. That gives them $37,150 ($72,500 - $35,350) that they could take from their IRA while staying within the 15 percent marginal bracket.

Let's take a look, on the next page, at what it looks like on a sample Form 1040 U.S. Individual Tax Return.

---

1. Based on tax year 2013 tax tables. These brackets are adjusted annually for inflation by the Internal Revenue Service.

Form **1040**	Department of the Treasury—Internal Revenue Service (99) **U.S. Individual Income Tax Return**	20**13**	OMB No. 1545-0074	IRS Use Only—Do not write or staple in this space.

For the year Jan. 1–Dec. 31, 2013, or other tax year beginning , 2013, ending 20 | See separate instructions.

Your first name and initial	Last name		Your social security number
If a joint return, spouse's first name and initial	Last name		Spouse's social security number

Home address (number and street). If you have a P.O. box, see instructions. | Apt no. | ▲ Make sure the SSN(s) above and on line 6c are correct.

City, town or post office, state, and ZIP code. If you have a foreign address, also complete spaces below (see instructions).

Presidential Election Campaign
Check here if you, or your spouse if filing jointly, want $3 to go to this fund. Checking a box below will not change your tax or refund. ☐ You ☐ Spouse

Foreign country name	Foreign province/state/county	Foreign postal code

Filing Status

Check only one box.

1. ☐ Single
2. ☐ Married filing jointly (even if only one had income)
3. ☐ Married filing separately. Enter spouse's SSN above and full name here. ▶
4. ☐ Head of household (with qualifying person). (See instructions.) If the qualifying person is a child but not your dependent, enter this child's name here. ▶
5. ☐ Qualifying widow(er) with dependent child

Exemptions

If more than four dependents, see instructions and check here ▶ ☐

6a ☐ Yourself. If someone can claim you as a dependent, do not check box 6a
b ☐ Spouse

c Dependents:	(2) Dependent's social security number	(3) Dependent's relationship to you	(4) ✓ if child under age 17 qualifying for child tax credit (see instructions)
(1) First name Last name			☐
			☐
			☐
			☐

Boxes checked on 6a and 6b __
No. of children on 6c who:
• lived with you __
• did not live with you due to divorce or separation (see instructions) __
Dependents on 6c not entered above __
Add numbers on lines above ▶ __

d Total number of exemptions claimed

Income

Attach Form(s) W-2 here. Also attach Forms W-2G and 1099-R if tax was withheld.

If you did not get a W-2, see instructions.

7	Wages, salaries, tips, etc. Attach Form(s) W-2		7	
8a	Taxable interest. Attach Schedule B if required		8a	10,000
b	Tax-exempt interest. Do not include on line 8a	8b		
9a	Ordinary dividends. Attach Schedule B if required		9a	
b	Qualified dividends	9b		
10	Taxable refunds, credits, or offsets of state and local income taxes		10	
11	Alimony received		11	
12	Business income or (loss). Attach Schedule C or C-EZ		12	
13	Capital gain or (loss). Attach Schedule D if required. If not required, check here ▶ ☐		13	
14	Other gains or (losses). Attach Form 4797		14	
15a	IRA distributions	15a	b Taxable amount	15b	
16a	Pensions and annuities	16a	30,000	b Taxable amount	16b	30,000
17	Rental real estate, royalties, partnerships, S corporations, trusts, etc. Attach Schedule E		17	
18	Farm income or (loss). Attach Schedule F		18	
19	Unemployment compensation		19	
20a	Social security benefits	20a	30,000	b Taxable amount	20b	15,350
21	Other income. List type and amount		21	
22	Combine the amounts in the far right column for lines 7 through 21. This is your **total income** ▶		22	

Adjusted Gross Income

23	Educator expenses	23		
24	Certain business expenses of reservists, performing artists, and fee-basis government officials. Attach Form 2106 or 2106-EZ	24		
25	Health savings account deduction. Attach Form 8889	25		
26	Moving expenses. Attach Form 3903	26		
27	Deductible part of self-employment tax. Attach Schedule SE	27		
28	Self-employed SEP, SIMPLE, and qualified plans	28		
29	Self-employed health insurance deduction	29		
30	Penalty on early withdrawal of savings	30		
31a	Alimony paid b Recipient's SSN ▶	31a		
32	IRA deduction	32		
33	Student loan interest deduction	33		
34	Tuition and fees. Attach Form 8917	34		
35	Domestic production activities deduction. Attach Form 8903	35		
36	Add lines 23 through 35		36	
37	Subtract line 36 from line 22. This is your **adjusted gross income** ▶		37	55,350

For Disclosure, Privacy Act, and Paperwork Reduction Act Notice, see separate instructions. | Cat. No. 11320B | Form **1040** (2013)

Form 1040 (2013)						Page 2
Tax and Credits	38	Amount from line 37 (adjusted gross income)			38	55,350
	39a	Check if: ☐ You were born before January 2, 1949, ☐ Blind. ☐ Spouse was born before January 2, 1949, ☐ Blind. Total boxes checked ► 39a				
Standard Deduction for—	b	If your spouse itemizes on a separate return or you were a dual-status alien, check here► 39b ☐				
	40	Itemized deductions (from Schedule A) or your standard deduction (see left margin)			40	12,200
• People who check any box on line 39a or 39b or who can be	41	Subtract line 40 from line 38			41	43,150
	42	Exemptions. ~~If line 38 is $150,000 or less, multiply $3,900 by the number on line 6d. Otherwise, see instructions~~			42	7,800
	43	Taxable income. Subtract line 42 from line 41. If line 42 is more than line 41, enter -0-			43	35,350

By withdrawing the IRA money when they didn't "have to" do so, this couple has actually taken advantage of a huge opportunity: 15 percent is by far the lowest tax rate these dollars will ever see. How ironic that so many people who focus diligently on sheltering their income from taxes during the "First Half" then expose that same money to unnecessarily high tax rates during the "Second Half!"

Let's say that same couple has $1 million in their IRA. At age 70 ½, they are going to be required to withdraw $36,497 as their RMD, based on 2013 IRS RMD calculations. That income will, of course, have a significant impact on their tax return.

First of all, because of this distribution, 85 percent (rather than 50 percent) of their Social Security income is now taxable. Along with their other income, including the RMD, their adjusted gross income is now $101,997. After subtracting their standard deduction of $12,200 and their exemptions of $7,800, their taxable income is now $81,997.

Remember, the 15 percent bracket for a married couple filing jointly stretches up to $72,500 as of 2013. But their taxable income of $81,997 now puts them in the 25 percent marginal tax bracket. This problem will only get worse: every year the RMD divisor decreases, which will increase the percentage of the IRA funds that they need to withdraw.

Let's take a look at that same sample Form 1040 U.S. Individual Tax Return, but this time showing the impact the RMD has on the taxable income:

Income

Attach Form(s) W-2 here. Also attach Forms W-2G and 1099-R if tax was withheld.

If you did not get a W-2, see instructions.

7	Wages, salaries, tips, etc. Attach Form(s) W-2		7	
8a	Taxable interest. Attach Schedule B if required		8a	10,000
b	Tax-exempt interest. Do not include on line 8a	8b		
9a	Ordinary dividends. Attach Schedule B if required		9a	
b	Qualified dividends	9b		
10	Taxable refunds, credits, or offsets of state and local income taxes		10	
11	Alimony received		11	
12	Business income or (loss). Attach Schedule C or C-EZ		12	
13	Capital gain or (loss). Attach Schedule D if required. If not required, check here ▶ ☐		13	
14	Other gains or (losses). Attach Form 4797		14	
15a	IRA distributions 15a 36,497 b Taxable amount		15b	36,497
16a	Pensions and annuities 16a 30,000 b Taxable amount		16b	30,000
17	Rental real estate, royalties, partnerships, S corporations, trusts, etc. Attach Schedule E		17	
18	Farm income or (loss). Attach Schedule F		18	
19	Unemployment compensation		19	
20a	Social security benefits 20a 30,000 b Taxable amount		20b	25,500
21	Other income. List type and amount		21	
22	Combine the amounts in the far right column for lines 7 through 21. This is your **total income** ▶		22	

Adjusted Gross Income

23	Educator expenses	23		
24	Certain business expenses of reservists, performing artists, and fee-basis government officials. Attach Form 2106 or 2106-EZ	24		
25	Health savings account deduction. Attach Form 8889	25		
26	Moving expenses. Attach Form 3903	26		
27	Deductible part of self-employment tax. Attach Schedule SE	27		
28	Self-employed SEP, SIMPLE, and qualified plans	28		
29	Self-employed health insurance deduction	29		
30	Penalty on early withdrawal of savings	30		
31a	Alimony paid b Recipient's SSN ▶	31a		
32	IRA deduction	32		
33	Student loan interest deduction	33		
34	Tuition and fees. Attach Form 8917	34		
35	Domestic production activities deduction. Attach Form 8903	35		
36	Add lines 23 through 35		36	
37	Subtract line 36 from line 22. This is your **adjusted gross income** ▶		37	101,997

Form 1040 (2013) — Page **2**

Tax and Credits

Standard Deduction for—
- People who check any box on line 39a or 39b or who can be

38	Amount from line 37 (adjusted gross income)		38	101,997
39a	Check if: ☐ You were born before January 2, 1949, ☐ Blind. ☐ Spouse was born before January 2, 1949, ☐ Blind. Total boxes checked ▶ 39a			
b	If your spouse itemizes on a separate return or you were a dual-status alien, check here ▶ 39b☐			
40	Itemized deductions (from Schedule A) or your standard deduction (see left margin)		40	12,200
41	Subtract line 40 from line 38		41	89,797
42	Exemptions. If line 38 is $150,000 or less, multiply $3,900 by the number on line 6d. Otherwise, see instructions		42	7,800
43	**Taxable income.** Subtract line 42 from line 41. If line 42 is more than line 41, enter -0-		43	81,997

When it comes to taxes, almost every person we've ever met simply completes his or her return, files it and then never looks at it again until next tax season. We also meet with countless individuals where there is a clear disconnect between the CPA who prepares their taxes and the financial advisor who manages their investments. In many of these situations, we find clear cases where tax savings opportunities are missed because no one is looking at the big picture and looking at strategies to minimize taxes.

There is no continuity between the two professionals – no one is looking at how to get the most out of your retirement, as opposed to only how to save a penny today even if it will cost you a dollar tomorrow. As we said earlier, that's why we like to quarterback the process. When everyone works together, everyone benefits.

REQUIRED MINIMUM DISTRIBUTION (RMD)

Required minimum distributions (RMDs) are the minimum amounts that must be withdrawn from a retirement account after its owner reaches age 70 ½. Failing to take these RMDs will result in stiff penalties from the IRS – as much as 50 percent of the required amount that you did not take out.

To determine the required minimum distribution, simply find your age on the government's "uniform lifetime table" (below), which gives you a certain divisor based on your age. For example, in your first year, when you turn 70 ½, your divisor is 27.4. If you have $1 million in your IRA account as of the previous year end, you divide $1 million by 27.4, which will give you an RMD of $36,496.

Age	Factor	Age	Factor	Age	Factor	Age	Factor	Age	Factor
70	27.4	80	18.7	90	11.4	100	6.3	110	3.1
71	26.5	81	17.9	91	10.8	101	5.9	111	2.9
72	25.6	82	17.1	92	10.2	102	5.5	112	2.6
73	24.7	83	16.3	93	9.6	103	5.2	113	2.4
74	23.8	84	15.5	94	9.1	104	4.9	114	2.1
75	22.9	85	14.8	95	8.6	105	4.5	115+	1.9
76	22.0	86	14.1	96	8.1	106	4.2		
77	21.2	87	13.4	97	7.6	107	3.9		
78	20.3	88	12.7	98	7.1	108	3.7		
79	19.5	89	12.0	99	6.7	109	3.4		

*IRS Publication 590

Each year, your divisor gets lower, which means the percentage you must withdraw increases. So the problem won't go away – in fact, each year it's going to get worse in the form of higher RMD withdrawal percentages. So withdrawing money prior to when the government says you must do so gives you a lot more flexibility and can save you a lot of money. We'll say it again: following conventional logic isn't always a good idea.

Over the next few chapters, we'll go into more detail about squeezing the brackets (getting money out at the lowest tax rate possible) and even share examples of how some people are able to withdraw money tax free.

Chapter 3 Dividends

1. Tax-deferred IRAs and 401(k)s are an effective way to build wealth, but they are also ticking tax time bombs.

2. The best way to defuse a ticking tax time bomb is with a smart income and distribution strategy.

3. A balanced distribution strategy aims to provide cash flow and extract retirement funds at the lowest possible tax rate.

4. Wait too long to withdraw funds, and the government's required minimum distributions (RMDs) could push you into a higher tax bracket.

Chapter 4

Early Retiree and Pre-59 ½ Strategies

"I had a very detailed retirement plan, and I feel like I've met every aspect of it: a lot of golf, a lot of carbs, a lot of fried food and some booze, occasionally. I've been completely committed... The results have shown."

— Andy Roddick, tennis player and winner of The 2003 U.S. Open

The best time to start preparing for retirement is as early as possible. One of the biggest mistakes we see many people make – even people who have tried to be rather responsible about their finances during the First Half of their financial lives – is that they start thinking about the Second Half when they are just a few months from it. Despite the fact that they've known all along that one day they would retire, it just doesn't become real until there's less than a year to go. So one of life's biggest wake-up calls is when it hits you: have I really prepared to the point where my family and I can have financial independence for the rest of our lives?

Even more to the point, most people have no idea what's involved in planning for retirement. They've adopted that conventional logic that says to put a small percentage of each paycheck into a company 401(k), and when they turn 65 years old everything will be okay, and they can spend the rest of their lives doing what they wish. Unfortunately, it's not that simple.

You need to make choices along the way, and being uninformed or misinformed can lead to financial devastation later on. Making the wrong decisions can end up costing you hundreds of thousands of dollars, not to mention the emotional toll of financial uncertainty.

Another big mistake people make: they say, "I do a good job adding to my company's 401(k) plan, and one of the big name financial firms is watching over the plan, so I'll be just fine." This is *your money* we are talking about. Don't believe your money is automatically safe and continuing to grow just because a big-name firm handles the plan administration. The reality: these cookie-cutter investment options are set up for the masses. They're not tailored to your situation. In addition, although not all financial advisors at these companies are leading you down the wrong path, the reality is that many of them are paid different commissions based on where they convince you to invest your money. What's best for them might or might not also be best for you.

Make sure your financial advisor is someone with whom you feel comfortable and someone who is knowledgeable. Remember, it's not just about putting as much money away as possible. It's also about knowing what to do with that money – where to invest it and how to properly manage it. Retirement planning has many little ins and outs, and not taking advantage of them at the right times can cost you dearly. Perhaps one of the best examples of this is when you're an early retiree or need cash quickly because of an emergency situation. Making the most of those pre-59 ½ strategies can have a drastic impact on your cash flow. It's at these times that conventional logic can actually work against you.

What happens when all of a sudden you need money for some reason, and every single dollar you have is in your retirement accounts? If you're under 59 ½, the answer isn't straightforward – and you need to overcome some hurdles. In addition to paying the income tax on the money you withdraw, just as you would have to do later, the government is going to impose a 10 percent early distribution penalty.

But in some cases, the IRS will allow you to pull money from a retirement account prior to 59 ½. You will still have to pay the income tax, but you won't have to pay that 10 percent early distribution penalty.

The most common scenarios:

- To purchase a first home ($10,000 lifetime limit)
- Higher education expenses
- To help pay health insurance premiums during certain periods of unemployment
- To meet certain unreimbursed medical expenses in excess of 7.5 percent of your annual adjusted gross income
- Upon death or disability
- To pay an IRS levy against your IRA
- As part of a series of substantially equal periodic payments (these are called "72(t) distributions.")

Most of these scenarios deal with a hardship, or they occur when people haven't done a good job of saving, and all of a sudden they need extra money and have nowhere else to turn.

Our clients who are trying to take money out of their retirement accounts prior to age 59 ½ are doing so for one reason: they're looking to retire early and provide themselves with retirement income. They already have the assets to live comfortably in retirement, but all their money is locked away in a 401(k) or IRA.

In certain situations and with the right financial planning, you can get the money out. In this chapter, we're going to discuss four of these options:

- Over 55 and separated from service
- Section 72(t)
- After-tax contributions
- In-service distribution option

OVER 55 AND SEPARATED FROM SERVICE

If you are age 55 or over and separated from service from an employer after you turned 55, you have the ability to take money out of that employer's retirement account without having to pay the 10 percent early distribution penalty. However, if you left another company prior to age 55, and then left your most recent employer after age 55, you can only withdraw funds from plan at that most recent employer – the one you left after you turned 55 – without penalty. If you left a previous company at age 49, for example, and then left your more recent employer after you turned 55, you would be assessed the 10 percent penalty for withdrawing funds from the plan at the company you left when you were 49.

One important thing to realize is that you lose this age 55-to-59 ½ penalty-free withdrawal ability if you roll funds from a 401(k) into an IRA, as many people do after they leave a company. So if we have a client who 1) is going to be retiring early and 2) has a large amount of money in retirement accounts, we'll often roll the majority of their assets into a IRA with us and strategically leave a portion of those assets in the previous employer's 401(k) plan just because it can be used as a backup cash reserve: they can tap those funds without any penalties. They still have to pay taxes regardless of when the money comes out, but they avoid any other penalties.

SECTION 72(t)

With any retirement account such as an IRA or 401(k), Internal Revenue Code Section 72(t) allows you to take money out prior to age 59 ½ and avoid the 10 percent tax penalty, provided that those distributions are taken as "substantially equal periodic payments." To avoid the 10 percent tax penalty, the periodic payments need to continue for the longer of five years or until you reach age 59 ½ (in other words, potentially into your 60s). This gives you a chance to access your money while avoiding the penalty. But it locks you in.

Let's say you're 50, and you get laid off and have money in an IRA. You can take equal periodic distributions to avoid the 10 percent early distribution penalty. Now let's say after two years you find a new job and no longer need the money from your IRA. The IRS will say: too bad. You must continue taking those distributions for another seven years, or the 10 percent penalty becomes retroactive, and you're forced to pay it on all your previous withdrawals from the past two years. There's no negotiating your way out of it. Worst of all, now that you're employed again, the withdrawals for the next seven years will probably be taxed at a higher rate than the ones during the years when you weren't employed and had little other income, keeping you in a lower tax bracket.

So although section 72(t) is a great vehicle and can provide you with income when you need it most, you need to think twice before using it. Weigh the risks and benefits. Think not only about your immediate situation but also about what the tax and cash flow impact will be if you take these distributions for as long as you will be required to take them. Bottom line: once you start a 72(t), you're stuck with it for the greater of the next five years or until you reach 59 ½, whether you need the money or not. An unwise choice could dent your retirement before you even reach retirement age.

The IRS provides three acceptable ways for calculating your "substantially equal periodic payment:"

- **Required minimum distribution method:** takes your current balance and divides it by your single life expectancy or joint life expectancy.

- **Fixed amortization method:** amortizes your account balance over your single life expectancy, the uniform life expectancy table or joint life expectancy with your oldest named beneficiary.

- **Fixed annuitization method:** uses an annuity factor to calculate your payment.

As complex as a section 72(t) distribution can be, the good news is the government gives you some choices in calculating your payment.

Even more good news: the government also allows you to calculate your 72(t) payments based on one or more of your IRA accounts. One of the biggest drawbacks to 72(t) distributions is that once they are started, you are locked in. So the added flexibility of being able to apply this strategy to only a portion of your retirement assets, rather than to all of them, is very helpful.

Typically, when considering whether to use a 72(t) distribution strategy for a client, we will do everything possible within IRS guidelines to use the smallest amount of their retirement assets to generate the maximum cash flow from these assets over the needed timeframe.

Bobby and Jan are a great example of how a Section 72(t) can help. They were both 55 years old and worked for a very successful pharmaceutical company. They wanted to retire early, but just about all their money was locked inside retirement accounts. They thought that if they retired at age 55, not only would they have to pay the taxes on any withdrawals, but they would also get caught paying the 10 percent early distribution penalty as well.

Well the only thing Bobby and Jan disliked even more than their jobs was paying income taxes. To lose an extra 10 percent of that money just wasn't an option. In this case, we took advantage of the 72(t) distributions and designated a portion of their IRA assets for those periodic income streams. This enabled them to get the money out of their retirement account prior to age 59 ½ without the 10 percent early distribution tax penalty.

Another couple we're working with is looking to retire at age 55 with no pension or any other income. We'll have to pull money from their retirement accounts to provide for their lifestyle. We will roll a large majority of their 401(k) assets into an IRA to give us more flexibility with their investments beyond the limited options within the 401(k), but we're going to strategically leave a portion of their savings in the 401(k) so that we can take out the money they need to live between 55 and 59 ½ without having to worry about any kind of restrictions.

Clearly, over 55 and separated from service is the preferable scenario, because it gives you maximum flexibility. Taking advantage of Section 72(t) is possible, but it leaves fewer options because it's more restrictive once the payments are set up. We typically look at the 72(t) option as the last resort. (Each of our client's circumstances is unique, and we make sure to review every aspect of clients' situations before making a suitable recommendation on a distribution strategy. Be sure you discuss your specific circumstances with your financial advisor before making any decisions.)

AFTER-TAX CONTRIBUTIONS – the 401(k) option you've probably never heard of (or maybe don't remember!)

Forbes called it "The 401(k) option you've probably never heard of," and that's because... well... most people indeed don't even know it exists. We're talking about making after-tax (rather than the far more common pre-tax) contributions to a retirement account such as a 401(k).

With after-tax contributions, the money is taxed before it goes into a retirement account. At the time you withdraw these contributions, you will be taxed only on the gains; after all, you've already paid income tax on the amount of the contributions themselves.

One of the biggest challenges we see with many retirees is that all of their money is in retirement accounts. This worked well for them during the savings and accumulation phase of their lives, but now that they are retired, they will run into a big tax problem if for any reason they need to tap a large portion of their assets at once. As we discussed in Chapter 3, withdrawing a lot of retirement savings at once can push you into a higher income tax bracket.

Because of this challenge, we are constantly looking for ways to get money out of our client's retirement assets with minimal or no tax liability. The "after-tax" contribution portion of a person's 401(k) provides us with a great opportunity we don't want to miss.

If we are doing a rollover for someone who has $30,000 in after-tax contributions in a 401(k), we can get that money out of the 401(k) without any tax consequences: that $30,000, after all, is simply a return of their initial after-tax investment.

We have two good options at this stage of the rollover call. If the person needs the money for some reason (say, a big purchase or because they just got laid off and need the extra cash flow) we can simply have the 401(k) plan issue a separate check for $30,000 to the individual – with zero tax impact.

Another option: to roll the after-tax contributions of $30,000 directly into a Roth IRA, which will now allow those assets to grow completely tax-free (yes, *tax-free*, not merely tax-deferred). That money will now be available for lump-sum distributions during retirement, if needed, with absolutely no tax consequences provided only the contributions are withdrawn and the gains remain within the account until age 59 ½.

We often refer to after-tax 401(k) contributions as "the forgotten benefit." In countless scenarios, before we call for the rollover, many individuals tell us confidently that they do not have any after-tax contributions in their plan – only for us to find out that the client has tens of thousands of dollars of after-tax contributions that they simply had forgotten about!

It is critically important to make the right decision with these after-tax dollars at the time of the rollover, because if these assets are rolled over to an IRA and comingled with the before-tax portion of the assets, you immediately lose the ability to get the lump sum with no tax consequences.

IN-SERVICE DISTRIBUTION OPTION

Many company retirement plans offer an "in-service distribution option," which allows participants to roll money out of their 401(k) and into an IRA account while they are still working. Many individuals look to do this to provide themselves with broader investment options than are available inside the company retirement plan.

This is perhaps one of the best strategies for having more control of your money – and it's one most people have never heard of. When we mention this option to our clients, many are surprised to hear it exists. And although it's not the right solution for everybody, most of the big-name firms don't tell people about it because they don't want them to take the money out of their own institutions.

Every company plan is different, so check with your plan's provider or review the plan documents to see what the options are. Some plans will offer in-service distribution options at any age, while others will not allow it at all. Many offer something in between: in-service distribution for participants who are over the age of 55, for example, or sometimes only those over age 59 ½. Some plans, meanwhile, will set a limit on the amount of money in a 401(k) that is available for in-service distribution.

From a tax perspective, people can roll the money out of their 401(k) accounts and into an IRA with no tax consequences and give themselves access to broader investment options.

Let's say you have $100,000 in your 401(k), and $30,000 of this is money you contributed as after-tax contributions. And let's say you have access to an in-service distribution, so you can roll it out, and you don't need that money to live. You can roll that $30,000 of after-tax contributions directly from a 401(k) to a Roth IRA at zero taxes (this Roth money now grows tax-free rather than merely tax deferred) and roll the remaining $70,000 into an IRA account with no tax consequences. (This $70,000 money continues to grow tax-deferred.)

For many of our clients who are still working, we have been able to use the in-service distribution option to better prepare them for retirement by starting to reallocate a portion of their 401(k) to an investment strategy more specifically focused on income and distribution.

A BALANCED APPROACH TO SAVINGS

In an ideal world, every person would have a good portion of savings outside retirement accounts as well as savings inside retirement accounts. This situation provides individuals with great flexibility to meet their cash flow needs in retirement, while at the same time reducing the tax impact on IRA distributions.

While most of our time with clients is spent helping them get money out of their retirement accounts at low tax rates, we also make sure our clients are making the right decisions when it comes to continued savings.

We recently met with a prospective client who was in the winding-down stage of his career. He had been laid off from his career job at a large manufacturing company, where he earned about $150,000 annually, and was now working at a $50,000-per-year job. He and his wife were living comfortably off his current $50,000 salary, and most of their savings were in IRA assets totaling about $1 million. He was continuing to maximize his 401(k) contributions, which might seem logical enough.

But here again, conventional logic does not work, because he is earning $50,000 annually. Because of deductions, their taxable income was about $30,000, which puts them well within the 15 percent marginal tax bracket with plenty of room to spare. Why, at the end of your working career, would you want to put money away at a tax savings rate of 15 percent when you know – with a high degree of certainty – you will never get that money out at less than a 15 percent tax hit? Following conventional logic does not work in this situation.

We had him reduce his 401(k) contributions to 3 percent, which was the percentage to maximize the company match on his 401(k) – turning down that "free money" is almost never wise. But he then saved the difference on an after-tax basis, giving him lump-sum-accessible money in retirement. As for the $1 million in IRA assets, we began converting as much of it as we could – that is, as much as possible without pushing them out of the 15 percent bracket – to Roth IRA assets.

Remember, conventional logic has its time and place. But it's not always the right philosophy. Make sure your CPA, CFP® and financial advisor are working together to ensure your money is where it needs to be. This almost never happens, even though it makes sense for so many different reasons.

Preparing to have the right cash flow in retirement is a balancing act, and it means making the right decisions at the right times to ensure you and your family will be able to truly enjoy those golden years.

Chapter 4 Dividends

1. Retirement involves big sums of money. Not paying attention to the details can have severe financial consequences.

2. You can withdraw money without penalty from IRAs and 401(k)s before age 59 ½. But doing so comes with strings attached and must be done carefully.

3. The after-tax portion of a 401(k) can be a good opportunity to access retirement accounts with no tax consequences.

4. The conventional logic of socking away as much money in tax-deferred accounts as possible isn't always the best decision.

Chapter 5

59 ½ to 70 1/2 : Slow and Steady IRA Distributions Win the Race

"A man with a surplus can control circumstances, but a man without a surplus is controlled by them, and often he has no opportunity to exercise judgment."

-Harvey Firestone

We've already established how following conventional logic can often steer you toward the wrong decision – and how in retirement, following that conventional logic can cost you a fortune. Between the ages of 59 ½ and 70 ½, we see more people following this conventional logic than during any other time of retirement. And unfortunately, many people come to us once it's too late, when there's no way to reverse the damage that's been done.

Once you turn 59 ½, the government allows you to take distributions from your retirement accounts without penalties. You do, however, have to pay taxes on it when you withdraw it – whatever you withdraw is considered income. Of course, you also have the choice to leave the money in those retirement accounts, allowing continued tax-deferred growth. Most people believe that if they don't need the money to live, there's no reason to withdraw the money now and pay the taxes on money they don't need. They believe the best thing to do is leave the money in the accounts to allow for continued tax-deferred growth.

Seems logical, right?

But following this conventional logic with which we've all been brainwashed — leaving the money in these accounts to grow tax deferred — can cost you dearly. The problem arises when you turn 70 ½ and the government makes you start taking required minimum distributions (RMDs). The older you get, typically the more money you are required to withdraw, which means you have to report more income on your tax return. In many cases, this income can push you into a higher tax bracket.

For many of our clients, we have found through additional analysis that they end up paying a lot less in income taxes throughout their full retirement if they take some distributions out of their IRAs prior to age 70 ½ even if they don't need the money to live. Paying a few dollars in taxes today, in other words, could save far more dollars later.

Remember, IRA distributions can be a one-time lump sum, or they can be a series of distributions over a number of years. If the balance in the IRA is rather large, it almost never makes sense to withdraw it all at once because a big withdrawal could potentially push you into a higher tax bracket. Some people realize that. What far fewer people realize is that by strategically planning certain distributions at periodic intervals between the ages of 59 ½ - 70 ½, you can save a lot of money in the long run.

John and Donna were both 60 years old and recently retired when we first met them. They were living comfortably off a small pension that Donna was receiving. They also had a nice portfolio of non-retirement assets that they could draw from if necessary. They were in a low tax bracket at the time and because they weren't yet 62, they couldn't have even chosen to collect Social Security. But we wanted to do some long-term planning to make sure they wouldn't get buried in taxes when they turned 70 ½. And indeed, that's exactly what would have happened had they let the money just sit there. John and Donna, like most people, believed they should just let the money continue to grow tax deferred. But after we explained what would happen once they turned 70 ½, they understood why it was important to withdraw some of the money now.

Sure, they didn't need the retirement account money to live right now. But leaving it in there until age 70 ½ would have thrown them into a higher tax bracket. Because of their situation, we were able to get about $30,000 annually out of their IRA accounts and have it taxed at 15 percent. It doesn't matter that they didn't need the money. They were actually helping to preserve their wealth by getting it out of what – despite all their legitimate "First-Half" benefits – had now become tax-inefficient IRAs. Had they followed conventional logic and just let the money sit in those retirement accounts, they would have paid for that mistake down the road in the form of higher taxes. In their situation, a larger portion of their RMDs at 70 ½ would have been taxed in the 25 percent marginal tax bracket. That's an additional 10 percent in taxes they would have paid by waiting to take distributions.

The unconventional but superior logic here: if you have an opportunity to get the money out of a retirement account while you're in a lower tax bracket, doing so might make sense even if you don't need the money to live. Once you reach age 70 ½ and the government forces you to take RMDs, you could end up in a higher tax bracket, as would have happened to John and Donna.

1st Half Investments   ## 2nd Half Investments

Let's look at another hypothetical example. Say someone has $1 million in assets, with $200,000 of it outside an IRA and $800,000 of it inside an IRA. From the time they are 59 ½, let's say they need to draw $20,000 per year from their portfolio for living expenses. That $20,000 is coming from their non-IRA bucket so they can avoid paying the taxes. By the time they are 70 ½, and assuming there's no growth, the non-IRA bucket is now down to zero because they spent it all for their lifestyle. So now they have all their money inside an IRA account and not a single penny outside.

Now let's say they need $30,000 to buy a new car. Where are they going to get that money? In addition to having to withdraw the $20,000 annually from their IRA for their lifestyle, they are now going to have to withdraw $30,000 to buy the car. They've now dug themselves into a hole, because they are forced to take money from their IRA and pay the taxes on it at a higher tax bracket.

Had they avoided conventional logic and taken a series of distributions prior to age 70 ½, they would have had more flexibility and been able to put that money in other places, and it would have likely been taxed at a lower rate. That's why typically speaking, our general rule is if somebody can withdraw money from their IRA and have it taxed at just 15 percent, we're going to want to do that, because it's highly unlikely you're ever going to pay anything lower on that money when it comes out.

Another important reminder from this scenario: every year it's essential to look and see how much money you can withdraw without leaving the 15 percent bracket. One year it might be $12,500; the next year it might be $8,400. Everybody's situation is different, but the goal is to maximize it and pull out as much as possible without stepping into a higher tax bracket. This is another good reason why your financial advisor and accountant need to be on the same page.

2013 Taxable Income Brackets Structure (as reported by the IRS)

Tax Rate	Single Filer	Married Joint Filers	Head of Household Filers
10%	$0 to $8,925	$0 to $17,850	$0 to $12,750
15%	$8,926 to $26,250	$17,851 to $72,500	$12,751 to $48,600
25%	$36,251 to $87,850	$72,501 to $146,400	$48,601 to $125,450
28%	$87,851 to $183,250	$146,401 to $223,050	$125,451 to $203,150
33%	$183,251 to $398,350	$223,051 to $398,350	$203,151 to $398,350
35%	$398,351 to $400,000	$398,351 to $450,000	$398,351 to $425,000
39.6%	$400,001+	$450,001+	$425,001+

Retirement is a cash flow game. The key is to make sure you are getting that cash flow in the most tax-efficient manner.

By doing so, you are keeping more money in your pocket and out of the government's pocket, and this will provide you with more to spend on what you want to spend it on.

There's also a psychological aspect to all of this. The decision to rent that house on the Outer Banks for the entire family for a week – *and pay for everybody's travel expenses?* It feels easier if it only costs $10,000 from non-IRA money as opposed to having to withdraw $12,000 from an IRA account just to net $10,000. When you have control over your cash flow, you are able to better control your taxes. The goal is to attain more of a balanced approach to the distributions and the income stream.

The real key to winning the game and achieving that balance is looking at your tax return. Ninety-nine percent of people get their taxes done, put the return away and never look at it again. If you ask someone what tax bracket they are in or what their taxable income is, they usually have no idea. They know how much money they have in their IRAs and what the performance has been, but they have no idea what their taxable income is. Most people end up thinking they are in a higher tax bracket than they really are.

In other situations the person is clearly never going to get the money out of an IRA at less than the 25 percent bracket. It's different for everyone. To get money out at the 15 percent tax bracket in 2013, a husband and wife could have up to $72,500 in taxable annual income. If all the money is in IRAs and they use all their non-IRA money first to avoid paying taxes and then the husband or wife dies, now the surviving spouse is going to have to file as a single tax payer.

In order for that widow to stay in the 15 percent bracket, the threshold for his or her taxable income now drops to $36,250. If the surviving spouse is going to continue to live off, say, $60,000, it's suddenly a much more dire tax picture – remember, $60,000 is well within the 15 percent bracket for a couple but is well into the 25 percent bracket for a single taxpayer. And our experience during the past two decades has taught us that after your spouse passes away, you're not going to be able to live on half the income. Yes, your living expenses will drop once you're single. But because you're not sharing certain costs anymore, they won't likely be cut in half, and you won't likely be able to get by on $35,000, depending on your situation and lifestyle. If indeed you can't adjust your lifestyle to accommodate living on $35,000, you're going to pay much more in taxes.

Losing a spouse is bad enough: you have to deal with the grief and try to adjust to life without him or her. Your finances shouldn't have to be a concern during a difficult time like this. But all too often they are, because people choose to follow conventional logic. This scenario would play out completely differently had this couple started taking periodic distributions between the ages of 59 ½ and 70 ½. The surviving spouse would now have more non-IRA assets (your ready-access money) and much more financial flexibility.

At some point, one way or another, the money has to come out of these retirement accounts. The objective is to get it out at the lowest possible tax rate. Between the ages of 59 ½ and 70 ½, if you're not working, you're typically in a low tax bracket. That's especially true when someone retires early, at 60 or younger, before they start collecting Social Security. There's a window of opportunity to get money out. If you leave it in, reasoning that you want to enjoy tax-deferred growth, the money is going to come out in one of two ways:

- When you're 70 ½, you're going to be required to take it out, and (as discussed in Chapter 3) the older you are, the higher a percentage of your money you will be required to withdraw.

- You're going to pass away, and your kids are going to take the money out. Once both spouses die and the kids inherit the money, an even larger income tax hit comes into play. (More on this in Chapter 7.)

In both cases, the money is going to come out at 15 percent in a best-case scenario – but more than likely at a significantly higher tax rate, depending on the situation.

Most people don't realize they have control over their taxable income. They assume they just have to wait until age 70 ½ or die with the money in these accounts. Once you retire, you actually have lot of flexibility in controlling what's going to show up on your tax return – a lot more flexibility than you had back when you were working.

At some point, taxes will blow up those IRA accounts, so the unconventional but typically better logic is: slow and steady IRA distributions win the race. You want to be able to take the money out of your IRAs slowly and steadily to keep you in a lower marginal tax bracket, as opposed to having it come out as a lump sum, throwing you into a higher bracket.

SOCIAL SECURITY PLANNING

Social Security planning is, of course, an important part of the retirement planning process. In fact, Social Security is extraordinarily significant for the estimated 40 percent of all Americans age 65 or older whom it literally keeps out of poverty. But even for the rest, it's a key source of income.

Nine out of 10 Americans age 65 and older receive Social Security benefits, according to the Social Security Administration (SSA). On average, these recipients depend on Social Security benefits for about half their income.

It's difficult to say exactly how much money you will receive from Social Security, but the average monthly benefit for a retired worker is roughly $1,200. Even aside from the wages you earned during your working life, various factors – including your retirement age (i.e., whether you are retiring early or later) and whether you plan to work during retirement – affect the amount you will actually receive.

Our general rule of thumb with Social Security planning is that if you are retired and are at least age 62, take the money as soon as you can get it. You've been paying into the program long enough, and it's better to spend the government's money than your own money. However, depending on the situation, holding off until age 65 might make sense to provide more room for Roth conversions prior to full retirement age. Again, this is an important point to make: your tax guy and your advisor have to be on the same page, communicating and planning how best to utilize your cash flow to lower your taxes.

Cash flow is king in retirement. Everyone's situation is going to be different, but regardless of what they do, everyone will face one thing in common: tax consequences. The key is to look for ways to minimize those tax consequences. You have a great deal of flexibility with your money in retirement. You just need to balance your cash flow to get the biggest bang for your buck.

If you're between the ages of 59 ½ and 70 ½, look at where all your money is right now. Is it all tied up in IRAs, or do you have a significant amount of non-IRA assets? Are you following the conventional wisdom of the masses, which says if you don't need the money you're better off letting it sit and grow tax deferred? If so, you should revisit your retirement plan and think about starting to take some distributions now. You're going to pay the taxes eventually, so you might as well do so in the lowest bracket possible.

Conventional wisdom isn't all bad. But if you follow it during this critical time of your financial life, it could end up costing you a lot of money! Your parents told you to eat your peas and carrots, but you didn't. Your teachers told you to study hard, but you slacked off. This time is different. Finally, you have a chance to help yourself by defying the rules and ignoring what other people say you should do!

Chapter 5 Dividends

1. Sometimes taking more money than you need out of your retirement accounts could help you avoid paying higher taxes later.

2. A good rule of thumb: Withdraw as much retirement money as you can within the 15 percent tax bracket.

3. Having all your funds in tax-deferred retirement accounts leaves you vulnerable to higher taxes throughout your retirement.

4. Social Security decisions can also impact IRA distribution decisions.

Chapter 6

The Roth IRA: To Convert or Not to Convert?

"I have no use for bodyguards, but I have very specific use for two highly trained certified public accountants."

—Elvis Presley

To convert or not to convert? That truly is a question retirees should be asking themselves. The rules surrounding Roth IRA conversions actually changed back in 2010. Prior to the change, if you earned more than a certain amount, you could not do a Roth IRA conversion. Now everyone has the ability to do a Roth IRA conversion regardless of their income.

But should they?

Many people are familiar with the basics of a Roth IRA account and a Roth IRA conversion. Let's quickly review to make sure these simple, yet very effective, strategies we discuss in this chapter are fully understood and can be implemented. A few quick and basic definitions:

- **Roth IRA:** This is simply a type of retirement account where you do not get a tax deduction for money when you contribute it (in other words, it is funded with after-tax money). Once the money is in the account it grows tax free. That's right... not tax deferred. TAX FREE. The money and earnings in this type of retirement account will never be taxed. NEVER. This is a very powerful vehicle if it's used wisely. (There are, however, potential consequences for pre-59 ½ distributions.)

- **Roth IRA Conversion:** The basics of this strategy are that you take money out of your traditional IRA today and pay taxes on the amount taken out of the IRA at today's tax rate. The money goes into a Roth IRA, where it grows tax free forever. That's right – FOREVER. Any money or earnings ever removed from the Roth IRA account are never taxed. (There are, however, potential consequences for pre-59 ½ distributions.)

- **Roth IRA Contribution vs. Roth IRA Conversion:** A contribution is when you deposit earned income into a Roth IRA. The government limits how much you can contribute each year to a Roth IRA. (In 2013, the contribution limit was $5,500, or $6,500 if you were over age 50. If your income is more than a certain dollar amount, you might not be permitted to contribute anything.) A conversion, on the other hand, is when you take money out of your traditional IRA and move it to a Roth IRA. Currently there is **no limit** to how much you can convert in any given year. This is a very important point, so let's repeat it. *There is **no limit** to how much you can convert from a traditional IRA to a Roth IRA in any given year.* Many times we talk to people who believe they face limits to how much they can convert on an annual basis. The reality: there are limits on contributions, but there are no limits on conversions. The limits the government has put on Roth IRA contributions severely impact someone's ability to effectively use this vehicle through contributions. However, the absence of a limit on conversions provides a huge tax-savings opportunity for many retirees.

Most often what we hear from other financial planners, stock brokers, CPAs, tax preparers and clients is that they want to take advantage of a Roth IRA conversion for two primary reasons. It is probably safe to say that when the financial markets dipped back in

2008, almost everybody's retirement accounts dropped in value, at least a little. So the theory was: do the conversion at that time, while the investments were down and faced less of a tax burden when they were converted, and let them recover tax free in the Roth IRA account. Seems logical, right?

The other thing we often hear from people is that they believe income tax rates will more likely be higher, not lower, down the road, so they are looking to use a Roth IRA conversion as a hedge against future higher tax rates.

We would argue that at this point (2015) the market has fully recovered (at least for now). And we would agree that there is a much greater chance of income tax rates being higher, not lower, in the future. However, we are not too excited about making a decision to pay taxes today for what is nothing more than a potential benefit. The reality is there is no guarantee that either of these two things will happen, so think twice before taking a certain hit today in exchange for an uncertain benefit later.

But what if...

THE ZERO PERCENT TAX CONVERSION

But what if we can withdraw money from your traditional IRA, convert it into a Roth IRA and pay zero taxes? That obviously makes a lot of sense if you can pull it off! But how?

For this to happen, you need to have or create a situation on your tax return where your deductions are greater than your income. As unreal as this may sound, it happens, and it happens a lot more than you might think. The most common time this happens is if we have a client who is a business owner who has some operating loss carry-forwards, or possibly a client with some rental losses, which essentially gives them negative taxable income. Sometimes it is a client with high itemized deductions because of either charitable contributions or high medical expenses.

We did something a few years ago that was pretty unique and resulted in a huge tax savings for one of our clients, Barbara. A few years before Barbara met us, she had invested $500,000 outside her IRA. When the market tanked, that $500,000 became worth about $300,000. We had her liquidate the investment (remember, this was money outside her IRA), and because of the way the tax laws work for an investment outside an IRA, we were actually able to claim almost her entire $200,000 loss as part of her miscellaneous itemized deductions.

So guess what else we did? We converted about $200,000 of her IRA holdings to a Roth IRA, and she paid zero taxes on the conversion! It gets back to the whole idea of looking at your tax return and knowing what options exist. To be able to do it at zero taxes always makes sense. When these opportunities present themselves, it's important to recognize them and take full advantage. (Barbara's situation is unique, and we encourage you to discuss your circumstances with a tax professional and a financial advisor to determine if a similar strategy might work for you.)

Anything above zero percent tax, however, takes a little more analysis. Typically, our rule of thumb is that if we can get money out of the IRA at 15 percent, it makes a lot of financial sense to do it. In most cases, that money isn't coming out at less than 15 percent down the road. We've had a few situations where we've looked at someone's portfolio, income and lifestyle, and they are clearly not going to be able to get the money out at less than 25 percent during their lifetime. In those cases, a conversion at a higher income tax rate might make sense. Each situation is different and carries its own set of unique variables. That is why your tax advisor and your investment team need to communicate and work together. You can't prepare your taxes, file them and forget about them. You really need to evaluate your cash flow and taxable income each year to see if there is an opportunity to try to turn the tax table in your direction.

We talked in Chapter 5 about John and Donna. You might recall that we were able to get about $30,000 a year out of their IRA and have it taxed at 15 percent. Because they did not need that money to live, we converted that $30,000 each year to a Roth IRA, which will allow those assets the opportunity to grow tax free forever.

WE ARE TALKING ABOUT REAL MONEY HERE

Here are the 2013 Federal Tax Rate Schedules:

2013 Taxable Income Brackets Structure (as reported by the IRS)

Tax Rate	Single Filer	Married Joint Filers	Head of Household Filers
10%	$0 to $8,925	$0 to $17,850	$0 to $12,750
15%	$8,926 to $26,250	$17,851 to $72,500	$12,751 to $48,600
25%	$36,251 to $87,850	$72,501 to $146,400	$48,601 to $125,450
28%	$87,851 to $183,250	$146,401 to $223,050	$125,451 to $203,150
33%	$183,251 to $398,350	$223,051 to $398,350	$203,151 to $398,350
35%	$398,351 to $400,000	$398,351 to $450,000	$398,351 to $425,000
39.6%	$400,001+	$450,001+	$425,001+

If you look at the marginal rates for each filing status, you will see that they go from 10 percent to 15 percent, 25 percent, 28 percent, 33 percent, 35 percent and finally 39.6 percent. The marginal rate means taxable income above a certain dollar amount is taxed at the higher rate. So let's say your filing status is married filing jointly (MFJ) and your taxable income is $62,500. The 15 percent marginal bracket for MFJ goes up to $72,500, which means you have room to pull 10,000 from your IRA and have it taxed at 15 percent (because $10,000 would take your taxable income up to $72,500).

So what's the advantage of doing this? If that same $10,000 comes out later, at a time when your taxable income is more than $72,500, that means that same $10,000 will now be taxed in the 25 percent marginal bracket. That is an additional 10 percent in tax you will be paying on that $10,000, or an additional $1,000 that you would be paying in taxes. Can we all agree that it would be better to have that $1,000 in your pocket instead of in the government's?

TIMING IS EVERYTHING

A Roth IRA conversion needs to be done before the end of a calendar year for it to count for that year. For example, if you wanted to do a Roth IRA conversion so it would show up on your 2013 tax return, it would need to have been done by Dec. 31, 2013. This is very important, and it can be confusing, because a lot of people assume they can do it any time before April 15 of the following year, just as they can make IRA contributions for the previous year up until tax day. This is not the case for conversions. We cannot tell you how many times we meet with someone for the first time and look at their most recent tax return and discover that they could have done a Roth conversion in that year at low or even no tax. But the opportunity for that year has now been lost. There is absolutely no way to go back and do it retroactively.

Doing a Roth IRA conversion takes some planning. We always have a handle on what each client's taxable income is going to look like each year to allow us to identify Roth IRA conversion opportunities. Then toward the end of every year, we discuss the numbers together and – when doing so makes sense – we do the actual conversions.

The government does, however, provide you a good option in case your estimate is off a bit. Although it will not allow you to do a conversion for a previous year, it will allow you to do the opposite: reverse all or part of a conversion for a previous year. This reversal is called a "recharacterization" and can be done until the time you file your return for that year, including extensions.

So what is the best way to do this? Toward the end of the year, once you have a good handle on what your income will look like for the year, it is as simple as estimating what your taxable income will be that year. That will enable you to see how much conversion you can do at, say, either zero percent or 15 percent tax. You are dealing with estimates at this point, so you might end up finding, when you or your accountant prepares your actual return, that your numbers were a little off.

But remember the recharacterization option. Because you are dealing with estimates, and because you can reverse but not initiate a conversion retroactively, it is always best to convert a little too much, rather than too little, to make sure you don't miss any opportunities. If we later find out that we converted too much and some of that conversion is going to be taxed at a higher tax rate – say, 25 percent – we can simply recharacterize a portion of the conversion to get the taxable income on the return back down to exactly where we want it.

The challenge here is that most individuals and financial advisors simply do not have the tax expertise or background to go through this analysis. At this crucial part of the year, when you really need guidance, your CPA or tax preparer is probably knee-deep in 4,000 tax returns and isn't looking for that opportunity. We would be willing to bet that your financial advisor, on the other hand, has never seen (or asked for) your tax return. This is where it becomes very important to have a financial advisor who is well versed in income taxes and tax planning – or to, at a minimum, make sure your financial advisor and your CPA or tax preparer communicate on a regular basis.

HOW CAN A ROTH CONVERSION HELP MY RETIREMENT LIFESTYLE?

We want to be able to get money out of an IRA and into a Roth IRA at a low tax rate for several reasons. First of all, you have potential tax-free income in the future from the Roth IRA, because you already paid taxes on those dollars.

Secondly, Roth IRA assets are not included in your required minimum distribution (RMD) calculation at age 70 ½, which means you will not be forced to take as much out of your IRAs as you would if all the assets were still in traditional IRAs. In many cases, that extra income would force you into a higher tax bracket, causing you to pay more in taxes each year.

The other thing we find is that many individuals have the majority or maybe even all their assets inside retirement accounts. That served them very well during the First Half of their financial lives, when the goal was tax deferral and accumulation. But during the Second Half, it presents a major challenge: every time they need a single dollar, they will need to consider the tax consequences. What we have found throughout the years is that people are much less likely to spend their money (in other words, less likely to enjoy their retirement) if spending that money causes them to pay more in taxes.

Strategically, getting money moved from an IRA to a Roth IRA at low or even no taxes provides individuals with much more flexibility in their retirement lifestyle.

We always say taxes are the one variable that you can actually control.

For example, let's say you are married. Between pension and Social Security, the annual taxable income for you and your spouse turns out to be $62,500. Let's also say your total portfolio of $1 million in investment assets is in IRAs. And now let's say you need to buy a new car, and the car you want to buy costs $30,000. It's safe to say that with $1 million in assets, you can responsibly buy a $30,000 car. But wait: something will cause you to hesitate. If you pull $30,000 out of your IRA to buy that car, the first $10,000 will be taxed at 15 percent ($1,500 in tax). And the next $20,000? It'll be taxed at 25 percent. That's $5,000 more in tax. So that $30,000 car will also cost you $6,500 in tax. We have found that this additional tax does impact people's purchasing decisions in retirement, and that saddens us, because many of these same people did all the right things during the "First Half" to put themselves in a position to afford most of what they want during retirement.

Well let's say, on the other hand, you had been doing a Roth conversion strategy. Every year, you converted $10,000 from your IRA to your Roth IRA to take advantage of the 15 percent tax rate. Let's say that you had done that for five years and now have $50,000 sitting in a Roth IRA. That decision to buy the $30,000 car just became a lot easier, because you can now pull $30,000 out of your Roth IRA account with zero tax consequences (with $20,000 left over for the next purchase!) Whether it's a new car, a 50th wedding anniversary special trip or a desire to treat the entire family to a vacation, we see tax consequences impacting individuals' spending decisions in ways that should have been avoidable.

Now let's take this example yet one step further. Once this couple turns 70 ½, with $1 million in IRA assets, they will have to take about $36,496 as their RMD. The first $10,000 would be taxed at 15 percent, but the next $26,496 would be taxed at 25 percent. Had the couple carried out a Roth conversion strategy of converting $10,000 annually out of their IRA, not only would that money have been taxed at just 15 percent, but it also would have lowered their RMD because they would have less in their traditional IRAs because of the conversions.

A FEW OTHER ROTH CONVERSION PLANNING POINTS

A lot of people believe that if they are going to do a conversion, they need to convert the entire account. Don't be misled. This is definitely not the case! Often – as we saw in Chapter 5 with John and Donna (the couple who retired at 60 and didn't need their IRA money to live) – when we do a conversion, it's not a lump-sum amount. We're typically doing it over a period of time. It's usually smaller amounts of between $10,000 and $50,000 per year.

One question we often hear: If I'm over 70 ½ and I have to take out my required minimum distributions, can I still do a Roth conversion? The answer is yes. However, your required distribution amount (the amount you're required to take after age 70 ½) cannot be converted.

We have had situations where it made sense to convert an amount beyond the RMD. If we have $30,000 of room left in the 15 percent marginal tax bracket and the required distribution is just $20,000, it still gives us $10,000 to convert. Or in 2009, for example, to give people a little bit of a break, Congress passed legislation that suspended RMDs for the year. This was a huge windfall for all of our clients, because it provided a phenomenal planning opportunity. Without a government-imposed RMD, many of our clients over the age of 70 ½ were able to remain in the 15 percent marginal tax bracket. Because they didn't have to take a required distribution, we had them take a distribution anyway and convert it to a Roth IRA. For many of our clients, we were able to convert up to $50,000 from their IRAs to Roth IRAs. That money is now growing tax free forever!

Another opportunity we have seen: when someone loses their big-salary job and is laid off. Instead of earning $150,000 annually, they're living off unemployment benefits and drawing money from their savings, which means temporarily, their income is very low. We've seen this situation play out many times over the recent economic downturn. Losing a job might not exactly sound to most people like an opportunity. Still, why not make the best of an unfortunate situation? We took advantage. During that one- or two-year period when those people were out of work, we did Roth conversions. In some cases, we used their IRA assets to supplement their lifestyle, because we could do it very tax efficiently. The good news is that some of these people had

$500,000 to $1 million in their IRAs and did not have a financial need to go back to work. It was extremely important to take advantage of the low tax bracket in which they now found themselves. Remember, once these opportunities are missed, there's no chance to go back and get them.

IT'S A TEAM APPROACH

This is another reason why it's imperative to make sure you have a team of advisors guiding you along the way. Relying on just your CPA, who is only concerned about crunching the numbers and preparing your tax return, won't be enough. Meeting once in a while with your insurance agent won't cut it, either. And even if you have frequent contact with your financial planner, that – in a vacuum – is also the wrong approach. Everyone needs to be on the same team, making sure important opportunities are never missed. It's also important for each individual or couple to make sure they are meeting or speaking regularly with each person overseeing their retirement. Think of it this way: when your primary care doctor refers you to a specialist, that specialist usually reports back to the primary care doctor. It's crucial that everyone knows what's going on. Finding a financial advisory team with tax planning knowledge and expertise, in addition to financial planning, insurance and investment management, is a great approach.

Retirement is a cash flow game. You're going to need money for different things at different times. Some of it is going to be the income you take on a regular basis. Other times it will be money you need for a car, special trip or home repair. If all your money is in the IRA and you take a lump sum, you're going to take a very big tax hit. Taking additional money out of your IRAs when you can, rather than only when you need it, can be a very powerful and effective strategy. Getting that money into a Roth IRA, where you can access it with no tax consequences, can literally change your retirement lifestyle for the better.

Many retirees are often misinformed because of the advice they receive from the bigger financial firms of the world. The problem with these firms is that they're offering advice to the masses. Retirement is a very personal process.

As we discussed in Chapter 5, slow and steady retirement account withdrawal is usually the most tax-efficient way to manage your tax liability. So why isn't your advisor recommending that you convert tax-inefficient assets to Roth IRAs each year? Many think the CPA is handling it. But some tax preparers are too busy just trying to get through the day – trying to file one return and move to the next one – to step back and look at your personal long-term picture. Maybe your advisor can't give you tax guidance and/or doesn't have the knowledge or planning experience to give you advice about these opportunities. Whatever the reason, opportunities are missed, and when you miss the opportunities, you lose them forever.

Brokers, meanwhile, are not CPAs. They aren't looking at your tax returns. They don't have the knowledge and expertise to give the right kind of guidance and advice. Most of these companies actually have a disclaimer on their website: "We're not authorized to give you tax advice." Then what are you paying for? Their clients are getting shortchanged in a big way.

The other thing these firms do is drive home the mantra that you're a long-term investor. When you're 75 years old, are you really still a long-term investor? Even when you're just 65 and you need to generate an income stream, long term doesn't work. Their objective is to grab control of your assets and keep them there for as long as possible. But the advice they give isn't the best advice for most people. They like to say "long-term investor" just to justify lousy short-term performance.

We often joke about it, but it's true: we're one of the few financial planning firms that actually encourages our clients to take their money and spend it.* Did you notice the little asterisk(*)? Well our "fine print" is that we can only encourage you to do that if you have an income and distribution plan in place! After all, isn't that why you saved all these years? As long as you have a solid cash flow plan, you should withdraw the money out in the most tax-efficient way and enjoy it! Go rent the beach house or buy the new car. Go do what you want to do. These are your golden years. With the right financial planning along the way, they will truly feel that way.

Chapter 6 Dividends

1. Converting an IRA to a Roth IRA requires planning and analysis. It should involve your CPA and your investment advisor.

2. Under the right circumstances and with the right planning, IRAs can even be converted to Roth IRAs while paying zero taxes or penalties.

3. Roth conversions are often not one-time events. For many people, a strategy of slow and steady conversions makes sense.

Chapter 7

Reducing Taxes When Your Will "Matures"

"The only difference between death and taxes is that death doesn't get worse every time Congress meets."

—Will Rogers

In the world of personal finance, estate planning is a lot like politics or religion: nobody wants to talk about it. The reason, of course, is that estate planning – more than any other area of finance – hinges on one's own mortality. The financial advisors of the world are not clueless to people's discomfort. You can buy theft insurance, you can buy fire insurance and you can buy flood insurance. But when was the last time someone tried to talk to you about "death insurance?"

When I (Gary) started out as a CPA at one of the "big-six" accounting firms, one of my mentors called me into his office to talk about estate planning. (As I was the young guy in the office, he always called me "Kid", which I absolutely loathed.) The first thing he said was, "Kid, sit down. I want to tell you something. Whenever you talk about estate planning, don't ever use the word 'death.' Don't use the word, 'dying.' People don't like that. Instead use the phrase, 'when your will matures.'"

It was great advice that I used for a long time. But let's be brave, shall we? Because you're reading this book, you're obviously serious about your finances for the Second Half of your life. And the Second Half of your life, by definition, includes your death. There's no way around it. (If you found a way around it, you should be writing a book, not reading this one!)

So being serious about our finances, let's start with a serious question: When your will matures… Wait, sorry – old habits! When you die, where do you want the money to go? Not surprisingly, our clients typically tell us they want their money to go to their children or grandchildren. Perhaps more surprisingly, many prefer the money go to their grandchildren instead of their children. One client told us – in jest, we like to think – that his grandchildren were his reward for not killing his kids. But I digress. The point is, the two favorite places that people want their money to go are to the children and grandchildren. After the heirs come charities. Much, much farther down the list is having the money go to a nursing home, a long-term care facility or the Internal Revenue Service. Of course, that's not so surprising.

But where does the money typically go? Far too often it goes to the folks on the bottom of the list rather than those on top. The money goes to end-of-life care facilities or to the IRS, and what's left over might reach the heirs or charities. Why? Quite simply, it's because people who might be very good at First-Half strategies (accumulating wealth) too often neglect the Second-Half strategies (distribution of that wealth). It's not surprising, really. In fact, it's safe to say that almost nobody focuses on Second-Half strategies. But as you'll continue to see, Second-Half strategies are important.

Let's look at an example of how money can wind up in the hands of the government rather than in the hands of your heirs. Imagine a person named Tom who is age 72 and has done well at accumulating wealth. Tom is living comfortably off his pension and his Social Security, and he has a solid cash reserve of $45k in his checking account. But in addition to his pension and his Social Security, Tom, like millions of other Americans, dutifully funded an IRA, by way of a 401(k) during the 30 years before retirement. That IRA (or 401(k) rollover) is now worth a handsome $800,000, which he doesn't really need and wants to pass on to his daughter, Elizabeth. Elizabeth is a single mom, aged 41, with three kids ages 8, 5 and 3. After childcare, housing and grocery costs, there's nothing left from Elizabeth's salary as a nurse for college or retirement savings. Unless things change, Elizabeth will be knee-deep in tuition costs when she's 50 and unable to save for her future. That means she'll likely reach 60 with little to no retirement savings. And her kids, Tom's grandchildren, will likely have hefty student loans to pay back. For three kids in 2020, tuition alone could mean a staggering bill of $465,000 (public university) to $720,000 (private university), according to CNN/Money[1]. And 25 years from now, when it's time for Elizabeth's retirement, even $1 million will be considered meager. With savings from only her income, Elizabeth will likely have only a tenth of that. Elizabeth's financial needs are great, and they are growing.

Naturally, Tom would rather see his life's savings go to his daughter rather than to the government. Fortunately, he lives on his pension and Social Security. And he has $800,000 in an IRA that's untouched and probably will remain so: he doesn't need it to live. Although this is a nice problem to have, it's a problem nonetheless: the IRA is vulnerable to a large degree of taxation. For example, what if Tom suddenly dies? If he has followed the standard advice, the $800,000 will be passed on to a beneficiary, which he named as his daughter. So what's wrong with that? Being a traditional IRA, which was tax-deferred all these years, it is taxable when it's withdrawn. And if it's redeemed all at once (by the way, it doesn't have to be; see the sidebar on "Stretch IRAs") it would likely catapult Elizabeth into the highest tax bracket, which currently means it could be taxed at 39.6 percent! That's right: a woman who is barely getting by would be in a higher tax bracket than a lot of rather high-income people. It would amount to a whopping $316,800 in federal income taxes. And that doesn't include possible state and local income taxes, possible federal estate taxes and possible state inheritance/estate taxes. Now, receiving $400,000 to $500,000 is better than nothing. But it won't be enough for Elizabeth to stop working at 65 or even 70. And it won't leave Elizabeth much savings at all if she uses it to pay off student loans. Bottom line: it won't provide basic financial independence for Elizabeth into her later years.

So, what's to be done? As we said at the outset, this isn't your father's retirement. It's time to think differently.

A Bit of a Stretch

When children or grandchildren receive funds in an IRA from their parents, they actually don't have to redeem it immediately or all at once. Instead they can roll it over into what's called a beneficiary IRA or what has come to be known as the "Stretch IRA." If rolled over, it won't immediately impact that person's income. But no matter the age of the inheritor, he or she will be required to take annual required minimum distributions (RMDs), similar to the ones people over 70 ½ must take from their traditional IRAs, based on the inheritor's life expectancy. The IRS provides different divisor tables for Stretch IRAs. Those RMDs could lift the inheritor into a higher tax bracket, so stretch IRAs are often not the most tax-advantaged way to transfer wealth. Also, if we are talking about very large sums of money, they could be subject to estate taxes.

Stretch IRAs are a good idea in principle. But in practice, they're another story. Although one's parents might have had the best of intentions to have that money continue to grow tax deferred for their heir's retirement security, all too often we find there is a sudden bill to pay or a bigger house to purchase or another car to buy. In other words, in our more than four decades of combined experience, what we have found has been that the vast majority of people who inherit IRAs cash them out within the first 12 months of receiving the account. This is a very costly mistake to make that usually blasts the beneficiary IRA into the top tax bracket (39.6 percent in 2014). The only stretching going on here is Uncle Sam stretching his arm out to grab his share!

Don't get us wrong: IRAs – both Roth and traditional – are great for the First Half of your financial life. Sheltering your savings (and the earnings from that savings) from taxes is a fundamental way to build significant wealth. They are a critical First-Half strategy.

But in Tom's situation, where it appears he's not going to need all or much of his IRA money and he wants most of it to go to his heirs, not the government, there's another Second-Half strategy to consider.

Before we get to that strategy, here's a one-question pop quiz: What's the one asset class that, when set up correctly, can be passed to heirs tax free? If you said "life insurance," you're smart. You're also probably puzzled. Why are we talking about life insurance for a 72 year old? The financially savvy folks reading this book are rightfully thinking that life insurance is for young people. After all, the standard financial advice goes a little like this: Life insurance is used to replace your income stream if you die. It enables the beneficiaries (i.e., your family) to pay off the mortgage or pay for college educations. As you get older and your children (hopefully) become self-sufficient, the mortgage gets paid off and you and your spouse build a nest egg, the need for insurance dwindles. You become, in effect, self-insured.

That's not a bad approach for a 30 year old. But because of the way tax laws are set up, life insurance as an investment can serve us well in our later years. This requires a real paradigm shift, so let's walk through it.

Because he has crossed the 70 ½ age threshold, Tom is required by the IRS to begin taking annual distributions from that $800,000 (or face severe penalties). In fact, applying the IRS divisor tables, his divisor will be 25.6 (see the IRS 2013 chart below), which amounts to an RMD of $31,250 from his retirement account. Supposing his effective tax rate is 20 percent, Tom will pay $6,250 in taxes, and he'll net $25,000 from the distribution. So the question becomes: what do we do with that $25,000?

UNIFORM LIFETIME TABLE

Age	Factor	Age	Factor	Age	Factor	Age	Factor	Age	Factor
70	27.4	80	18.7	90	11.4	100	6.3	110	3.1
71	26.5	81	17.9	91	10.8	101	5.9	111	2.9
72	25.6	82	17.1	92	10.2	102	5.5	112	2.6
73	24.7	83	16.3	93	9.6	103	5.2	113	2.4
74	23.8	84	15.5	94	9.1	104	4.9	114	2.1
75	22.9	85	14.8	95	8.6	105	4.5	115+	1.9
76	22.0	86	14.1	96	8.1	106	4.2		
77	21.2	87	13.4	97	7.6	107	3.9		
78	20.3	88	12.7	98	7.1	108	3.7		
79	19.5	89	12.0	99	6.7	109	3.4		

*IRS Publication 590

If we're confident that Tom doesn't need that money to live, the reality at this point is that Tom will be reinvesting it for Elizabeth. So how will he (or his heirs) get the most bang for his buck? Believe it or not, very often the best answer is life insurance. Again, keep in mind, this is not about insurance in the usual sense.

We are approaching this entirely from a return-on-investment perspective, and as you'll see, life insurance can be a viable investment option.

Tom is starting with $800,000 in an IRA. At age 72, the IRS requires him to take a distribution of $31,250, minus $6,250 in taxes (assuming 20 percent), netting him $25,000. What if he could use that $25,000 to buy an $800,000 guaranteed life insurance policy? "What?" you might say. "Pay $25,000 a year for life insurance? That's crazy." Well, before we start throwing around words like "crazy," let's run the numbers.

Suppose Tom pays $25,000 a year for that policy for 10 years and dies at age 82. He will have spent $250,000 on life insurance, but his heir will receive $800,000 tax free. Yes, you read that correctly. Right away, we can see this is one strategy to beat the ticking tax time bomb. Remember, as we discussed earlier, if you have $1 million in an IRA, you really don't have a million dollars. Rather, you have a million dollars minus the taxes that have yet to be paid on that million. But taking at least some of that IRA money and converting it into life insurance is one way of defusing the bomb.

Also, in the 10-year scenario described above, not only would Tom's heir receive $800,000 tax free. He or she would still receive the remainder of the IRA, minus taxes. On the next page, we'll see how much that $800,000 would really end up being, assuming zero growth in the IRA, with Tom taking the required minimum distribution each year for 10 years, based on 2013 IRS figures.

Year	IRA Funds	IRS Divisor	Required Minimum Distribution
Year 1	$800,000	25.6	$31,250
Year 2	$768,750	24.7	$31,123
Year 3	$737,627	23.8	$30,993
Year 4	$706,634	22.9	$30,857
Year 5	$675,776	22	$30,717
Year 6	$645,059	21.2	$30,427
Year 7	$614,632	20.3	$30,277
Year 8	$584,355	19.5	$29,967
Year 9	$554,388	18.7	$29,646
Year 10	$524,741	17.9	$29,315

As you can see, Tom will leave behind roughly half a million taxable dollars in his IRA. Such an amount, if Elizabeth took it in a lump sum, would land her in the highest tax bracket, which would expose her to a tax rate as high as 39.6 percent. That would mean $196,000 would go straight to the federal government alone. Under this scenario, Elizabeth would receive something in the neighborhood of $300,000 from the IRA, plus the full $800,000 from the life insurance policy, bringing the after-tax total to $1.1 million. That's not bad considering we started with an $800,000 taxable IRA. That will enable Elizabeth to help her children and leave her some significant retirement savings.

Zilch... Zero ...Nada.

How would you like for the government to get nothing from your estate? It can be done with the right strategy. For example, we could set up your heirs (kids/grandkids) as beneficiaries of a life insurance policy, and they will receive the full life insurance death benefit ($800,000 in Tom's example) completely free from income tax, estate tax and state inheritance tax. If you then name a charity as the beneficiary of the IRA account, the charity will receive the remaining amount of the IRA account ($524,741 in the example) also completely free from income tax, estate tax and state inheritance tax. This powerful strategy makes clear the idea that your money will go somewhere. The question is: where do you want it to go? A little careful planning can mean that hundreds of thousands of dollars go to causes and people you cherish instead of to the government.

Now, what would happen if Tom followed the conventional path? Of course, he would take the required minimum distributions and pay the taxes on those each year. And after 10 years, his IRA would be in exactly the same place, $525,000, which would be roughly $325,000 after taxes. But how would he reinvest the $22,000 to $25,000 in after-tax distributions? With his relatively short time horizon, it would have to be something fairly liquid, low-risk and thus fairly low-interest. In today's environment, he would be lucky to get 1 percent. But let's be generous and give him 3 percent. Now, let's revisit the 10-year chart, adding in columns for Tom's new investments, the investment earnings on those investments and the taxes required on those earnings.

Year	IRA Funds	IRS Divisor	Required Minimum Distributions	RMDs after taxes (20%)*	Total investment based on 3% growth rate	Investment earnings only
Year 1	$800,000	25.6	$31,250	$25,000	$25,750	$750
Year 2	$768,750	24.7	$31,123	$24,899	$51,421	$1,523
Year 3	$737,627	23.8	$30,993	$24,794	$77,758	$3,065
Year 4	$706,634	22.9	$30,857	$24,686	$104,777	$5,398
Year 5	$675,776	22	$30,717	$24,574	$132,494	$8,541
Year 6	$645,059	21.2	$30,427	$24,342	$160,810	$12,516
Year 7	$614,632	20.3	$30,277	$24,222	$189,857	$17,340
Year 8	$584,355	19.5	$29,967	$23,974	$219,526	$23,036
Year 9	$554,338	18.7	$29,646	$23,717	$249,829	$29,622
Year 10	$524,741	17.9	$29,315	$23,452	$280,776	$37,117
					Total investment earnings:	$138,907
					Taxes to be paid on those earnings (20%):	$27,781

*Assumes 20% effective tax rate, a reasonable hypothetical

And so we see after Tom started with $800,000 in his IRA, the RMDs have still reduced it to $525,000, and his investment outside the IRA has grown to $280,000. However, Tom has to pay taxes on the $139,000 in investment growth along the way, which will amount to roughly $28,000. That money has to come from somewhere and could reduce the $280,000 to $252,000. So, Tom has roughly $777,000 to leave to Elizabeth, $525,000 in his IRA and $252,000 outside of his IRA. If we apply the highest tax rate (39.6 percent) to the $525,000 that needs to come out of his IRA and get taxed in the process, she will net $317,000 from the IRA assets and $252,000 from the assets already outside of his IRA for a total of $569,000. Remember, in the other example, the net was $1.1 million – a difference of $531,000! Yes, the *difference* is almost equal to the *total* amount she would receive under the second scenario.

For a lot of people, $531,000 is a life savings. But it can be lost through poor planning. As you can see, the "ticking tax time bomb" is an apt metaphor.

If you're like many of our clients, you're having an "a-ha" moment right about now. Very rarely do we come across someone who has ever considered this strategy. Why? Two reasons: The first is that too often people are still in the First-Half financial mindset. Rather than thinking about how to accumulate wealth, now they need to think about how to distribute their wealth. It's a difficult transition to make. Notice that in the two examples we just examined, only in the second example did we talk about investing, rate of return and earnings. Those are tools for accumulating wealth (First Half). They are less useful for distributing wealth (Second Half). Now don't get us wrong: it's important to have the right investments. However, understand that the investments are just a part of the overall equation. It goes to show you how it's a matter of switching to the Second-Half mindset. The second reason is that people have trouble imagining needing life insurance so late in their life. And in general, they're correct. A 72-year-old has no true need for life insurance. But in this instance he's not buying insurance for the insurance. Rather, he's buying an investment which has a tax advantage – and that tax advantage happens to be extraordinarily important when you're dealing with the huge dollar amounts typical of a 72-year-old saver and investor.

Of course, Tom's situation is just one example. Because everybody's situation is different, that leaves a number of questions. What if he died after 20 years instead of after 10? What if he died one year after taking out the life insurance policy? What if he couldn't get life insurance for that price? What about estate taxes?

Those are all reasonable questions, which we'll answer now. It sounds a bit macabre to say, but with life insurance, the sooner you die, the better a return on investment you get. Your beneficiary might receive a million dollars after you pay only one year of premiums! But what if you live a long time? This is a good question. Because of its tax advantages and its guaranteed benefits (no market risk, based on the claims-paying ability of the insurer), life insurance can still be a good option even if you live well into the policy period.

Consider the example of a couple, both age 70 and in relatively good health, who buy a joint life insurance policy (sometimes referred to as a survivorship policy or second-to-die policy) with a $1 million benefit and a $19,847-per-year premium. With joint policies, the death benefit is only paid out upon the death of both spouses. At age 70, this hypothetical couple's joint life expectancy (LE) is age 93, according to the CSO Mortality Table. That's the age when the second of the two is expected to die. But as you can see from the graph on the next page, their rate of return is still fairly attractive even if one of them lives beyond age 93. At age 94 the internal rate of return is still a healthy 5.5 percent, and if you factor in the tax savings, it's the equivalent of an 8.5 percent taxable return. Not bad for an investment that requires no market risk.

Life Insurance As An Asset

What are the Advantages of Life Insurance?

1) Life insurance death proceeds are typically paid income tax-free to the policy beneficiary

2) Life insurance policies owned by an irrevocable trust may avoid estate taxes

3) To equal the economic value of the life insurance death benefit proceeds, equivalent annual contributions into a taxable investment would require higher yields and possibly greater risk.

Client Assumptions		Policy Assumptions	
Policy Type: Survivorship		Premium	$19,847
Male	Female	Premium Years	35
Age 70	Age 70	1035 Exchange	$0
Preferred Non-Smoker	Preferred Non-Smoker	Death Benefit	$1,000,000
		Guaranteed Age	105
Joint Life Expectancy: 93		Income Tax Rate	35.0%

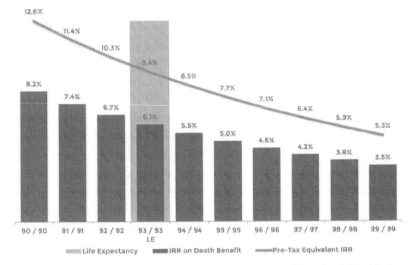

Chart by Highland Brokerage

Looking even a little deeper, if one of them survives until age 100 – a fairly unlikely[2] scenario – they'll have paid $595,000 in premiums, which sounds expensive. But upon the second spouse's death, their beneficiary will collect $1 million tax free. In other words, even if one of them outlives their LE by seven years, things still will have worked out.

Life Insurance as an Asset Strategy Snapshot

Year	Age	Scheduled Premium	Death Benefit	Internal Rate of Return on Death Benefit	Pre-Tax Equivalent Internal Rate of Return at 35.0%
1	71 / 71	19,847	1,000,000	4938.5%	7597.8%
2	72 / 72	19,847	1,000,000	561.6%	864.0%
3	73 / 73	19,847	1,000,000	230.6%	354.8%
4	74 / 74	19,847	1,000,000	133.7%	205.7%
5	75 / 75	19,847	1,000,000	90.2%	138.8%
7	77 / 77	19,847	1,000,000	51.2%	78.8%
8	78 / 78	19,847	1,000,000	41.0%	63.1%
10	80 / 80	19,847	1,000,000	28.3%	43.6%
12	82 / 82	19,847	1,000,000	20.8%	32.0%
13	83 / 83	19,847	1,000,000	18.1%	27.9%
15	85 / 85	19,847	1,000,000	14.1%	21.7%
17	87 / 87	19,847	1,000,000	11.2%	17.2%
18	88 / 88	19,847	1,000,000	10.0%	15.4%
20	90 / 90	19,847	1,000,000	8.2%	12.6%
22	92 / 92	19,847	1,000,000	6.7%	10.3%
23 LE	93 / 93	19,847	1,000,000	6.1%	9.4%
24	94 / 94	19,847	1,000,000	5.5%	8.5%
27	97 / 97	19,847	1,000,000	4.2%	6.4%
28	98 / 98	19,847	1,000,000	3.8%	5.9%
30	100 / 100	19,847	1,000,000	3.2%	4.9%

Joint Life Expectancy (LE) as used in this presentation shows the average age at death based on the ages and underwriting classes selected (preferred male, age 70 and preferred female, age 70). The Joint Life Expectancy illustrated in this presentation is 93 based on the 2001 CSO Mortality Table.

The hypothetical case study results are for illustrative purposes only and should not be deemed a representation of past or future results. This example does not represent any specific product, nor does it reflect sales charges or other expenses that may be required for some investments. No representation is made as to the accurateness of the analysis.

Any guarantees are subject to the claims paying ability of the issuing insurance company.

This material was created to provide accurate and reliable information on the subjects covered. It is not intended to provide specific legal, tax or other professional advice. The services of an appropriate professional should be sought regarding your individual situation.

For the sake of simplicity, in the examples above, we haven't yet talked about estate taxes. But for high net worth individuals, who could be vulnerable to estate taxes, using insurance as an asset class can be even more lucrative if it's inside or "owned by" an "irrevocable life insurance trust" or ILIT (pronounced "eye-lit"). An ILIT is a trust set up by an estate attorney for the purpose of owning a joint ("second-to-die") life insurance policy. Because the trust actually owns the insurance policy, it's no longer effectively owned by the insured and thus keeps the death benefit payout separate from the insured's estate value. Because it's outside the estate, the eventual benefit payout of this joint life insurance policy won't be exposed to federal estate taxes, state inheritance taxes or state/federal income taxes. Instead it passes through "triple tax free."

One of the reasons we recommend a joint policy is that it's generally cheaper to get insurance on two lives rather than one life. But that, of course, depends on both spouses being insurable. Often only one spouse is insurable, usually because of questionable health conditions. But to many people's surprise, this survivorship strategy can still work and be a very tax-efficient way to maximize your wealth transfer to the next generation.

For example, let's say the husband is uninsurable but the wife is able to get insurance in her name. She could have an estate attorney set up an ILIT with a provision where the spouse still can access the death benefit payout if needed (commonly referred to as a SLAT provision: spousal lifetime access trust). This SLAT provision allows her husband to access the death benefit if she dies before he does. The husband doesn't have to take the death benefit payout. If he doesn't need the money, he could have it continue to sit outside the estate, in the SLAT, with the same benefits the ILIT offered in a second-to-die policy, enabling the assets to ultimately transfer to the kids and grandkids triple tax free.

For those who already have an insurance policy in place, they can "gift it" to the irrevocable insurance trust with the caveat that you must outlive a three-year look-back provision. Translated into English, that means if your will "matures" within those three years, the policy is dragged back into your estate as if you never gifted it into the trust.

Occasionally neither spouse is insurable, or neither is in good enough health to get a reasonably priced policy. In such cases, you should have some candid conversations with your financial advisor about gifting and transferring assets to other irrevocable trusts.

One important note: While it's entirely possible to build a tax-efficient investment portfolio in the Second Half with the interaction of just a financial planner and accountant, when you start talking about finding ways to maximize the amount of assets you transfer to your loved ones, it becomes a team game. It is absolutely critical to have your advisory team – your estate attorney, accountant, insurance agent, and financial planner – all working together with the same plan.

We understand why using life insurance as an asset class is, for a lot of people, difficult to accept at first. But when you think about it, it really shouldn't be. In the Second Half of life, when we presumably have accumulated the most wealth we'll ever have, avoiding market risk and the ticking tax time bomb are paramount. Life insurance accomplishes both those goals and, if handled properly, it can help transfer large sums of wealth to children and grandchildren tax free. Maybe we need to just change the name from "life insurance" to a "wealth replacement tool."

[1] CNN/Money "Stop the tuition madness" by Kim Clark and Penelope Wang, Sept. 9, 2011

[2] According to U.N. estimates in 2012, the world had only 4.4 centenarians per 100,000 people.

Chapter 7 Dividends

1. Life insurance benefits can be passed to heirs tax free, and therein lies an opportunity.

2. Retirees often have no need for the insurance in life insurance, but it can be a valuable tax-advantaged investment.

3. Viewing life insurance as an investment requires a "Second-Half" mindset.

4. Estate planning and wealth transfer requires a team approach including a CPA, financial planner and an estate attorney.

Chapter 8

Do I Need A Trust?

"Put not your trust in money, but your money in trust."
— Oliver Wendell Holmes

James Bond had "Shaken, not stirred."

Dirty Harry had "Go ahead, make my day."

If estate planners had movie catch phrases, the one we'd choose would be: "Estate planning is about living – not dying."

We tell our clients that probably once a week. But what does it truly mean?

Most people think estate planning is about their death. But it's really not. Although it involves one's death, it's really – in a couple of fundamental ways – about living. First, most decisions regarding estate planning will wholly and solely impact the lives of your heirs, and it could affect them for decades. It's about their lives much more than your death. But estate planning, believe it or not, is also about your life. When most people sign a will, they don't keel over with the pen still in their hand. No, they go on living, usually for decades. But proper planning can start serving them along the way, providing confidence and perhaps some satisfaction that they've done the best they could for the people they care about. Estate planning isn't about dying. It's about your control over your assets – control while you're living, and control after your death.

One of the most basic ways to gain control is through a simple will. But for people with more complex concerns, a trust can also come in handy for controlling your assets. A lot of people think – probably because the term "trust fund" is usually associated with people like Paris Hilton – trusts are only for rich people. There's a bit of truth to that, but mostly it's false. The legal work to establish a trust can cost a few thousand dollars, so a trust doesn't make sense for everyone. If we're talking about a million dollars or more in assets, then the expense of a trust is less of a consideration. But with that said, it's really not the amount of wealth that drives the need for a trust. Rather, what drives the need for a trust is the level of control you want to maintain over your assets. A trust provides flexibility – even creativity – with that control that a will alone might not.

> **Another common misconception about trusts is that they provide an extensive tax shelter. Generally, having a trust won't save you or your heirs any more in taxes than basic estate planning will. In most cases, what drives the need for a trust is the level of control you want to maintain over your assets.**

As we'll see, trusts can help avoid estate taxes, but federal estate taxes only impact a fraction of 1 percent of the population. Estate taxes are a concern for the very wealthy looking to pass on well over $5 million in assets. People come to us all the time thinking they need a trust for tax purposes, but trusts generally aren't helpful with taxes. Again: trusts are about control issues – not tax issues.

What exactly is a trust? If you walk into a law library, you might find a definition that reads a little like this: "A trust is a legal arrangement in which a person's property or funds are entrusted to a third party to handle that property or funds on behalf of a beneficiary." So what does that look like in the real world? A typical example would be a parent who wants to leave assets to a child, grandchild or even a charity. The parent might establish a trust in which upon their death, certain funds will be held by a financial institution (that's the third party) to be distributed to the heir upon her 18th birthday. If that's too soon, the parent might decide that the child doesn't get the money until age 21. Or if the parent wants to ensure the child has a financial foundation well into adulthood, the funds might be dispersed in annual increments through age 30, 35 or 40 or whatever the parent decides. That's just one of many examples, but the power of a trust is already starting to emerge. That power is control.

In that example of a trust, the parent – the person who creates the trust – is known as the "settlor." The "trustee" can be an individual, an institution (such as a bank or trust company) or a combination of both. Usually it's one of the kids, an attorney or another trusted advisor. In most cases, the child or grandchild is the "beneficiary" of the trust (i.e., the one who ultimately gets to enjoy the benefits of the trust). The trustee is responsible for managing all of the property owned by a trust for the benefit of the trust beneficiaries. (That's important, and we will revisit that.) And the existence of the trust puts the trustee and beneficiary into a legal fiduciary relationship – one that's framed by the terms of the trust. Basically, the trust legally owns the trust's property, but only the beneficiary has the legal right to benefit from the trust.

Although that's generally how a trust works, trusts can come in many different shapes and sizes. For people who are serious about their Second-Half finances, looking at a few types of trusts and their purposes could help decide whether a trust would be of value. Trusts enable you to do things with your money – even after your death – that you might not have considered.

There are essentially two basic types of trusts when talking about estate planning. A living trust, also known as an "inter vivos" (that's Latin for "among the living") trust is, as its name suggests, a trust in which the settlor is still alive.

The second type of trust, a testamentary trust, doesn't take effect until after one's death. A testamentary trust is set up as a provision in a will and springs to life after the settlor's passing.

Living trusts can be either revocable or irrevocable. If it's a revocable trust, you can make changes. And such flexibility often can come in handy. A common example of where a revocable trust is advantageous is when someone sets up a trust and subsequently gets divorced. Or perhaps a beneficiary faces a major life change. A son or daughter could win the lottery, making the parent's money better valued elsewhere. Or a son or daughter could have an accident that leaves them mentally debilitated, which might necessitate the trust being restructured to funnel funds through a guardianship. Or perhaps a beneficiary, as he becomes a teenager, starts exhibiting irresponsible behavior that makes his parents doubt whether he'll have the maturity to receive a lump sum and would be better served receiving installments well into his adulthood. While some of these scenarios may be unlikely (who ever heard of an irresponsible teenager?), the point is: the randomness of life is all too certain. Circumstances change, people change, political winds change and the economy changes – all these are reasons to consider a revocable trust.

So, with that said, why would anybody choose an irrevocable trust? Why would they want to barricade themselves from what is likely a huge proportion of their wealth? Wouldn't that be the opposite of the promised control a trust supposedly delivers?

All those are reasonable questions, yet irrevocable trusts are quite common. What's the appeal? What makes an irrevocable trust so scary – the handcuffs themselves – also makes it attractive, believe it or not. With an irrevocable trust, the settlor gives up ownership (or title) of the property to the trustee. (That's not necessary with a revocable trust.) The settlor truly no longer owns it. At that point, to make changes the settlor would need to get the permission of the trustee and beneficiary. So what's so great about that?

As it turns out, there are a number of attractive reasons for not owning something. Because the trust property is no longer owned by the settlor, it's also no longer a part of the settlor's estate, so it provides a level of protection from taxes and other threats to your assets. For instance, in the case of divorce or bankruptcy, funds in an irrevocable trust likely wouldn't factor into a settlement. In short, an irrevocable trust can play an instrumental and hugely advantageous role in asset protection.

So, now that we understand what a trust is, the next question is, "What can you do with it?" The answer is pretty wide open, but there are a number of trust types for fairly common concerns – common enough where they've got a trust type created to solve them. Here are some of those concerns and the trusts that might help to address them:

Concern: You want to avoid estate taxes.

Solution: Credit Shelter Trust (CST)

For married couples with a sizable net worth, a "credit shelter trust" can help them, or more accurately their heirs, avoid estate taxes. Basically, both spouses write into their wills a provision setting up the CST. Upon the death of the first spouse, the CST springs to life and is funded up to the Federal estate tax exemption amount, which indexed for inflation is $5.34 million per person or $10.68 million per couple in 2014. Suppose the couple has a net worth of $12 million. Upon the death of the first spouse, $5.34 million would move into the CST, which would have a provision where the surviving spouse could utilize a small percentage of those funds for income. But because the funds were moved into a trust, they are no longer part of the estate. And when the second spouse dies, the funds in the CST can pass to the heirs free of federal estate taxes. So because of the CST we are now talking about the second spouse's estate of approximately $6.7 million rather than a $12 million estate. And of that $6.7 million residual estate, upon the death of the second spouse, he or she could shelter $5.34 million of the estate using the unified credit exemption amount. In the end, after both spouses die, only $1.3 million of the original $12 million is subject to estate taxes.

Concern: You want to avoid estate taxes and income taxes for your heirs.

Solution: Irrevocable Life Insurance Trust (ILIT)

We talked about the ILIT in Chapter 7, but an ILIT is another example of the power of how an irrevocable trust can provide asset protection. You'll recall that because the life insurance policy is in an irrevocable trust, it's not part of the estate and thus will avoid estate taxes. Meanwhile, payouts from life insurance policies are exempt from income taxes, so they pass to the heirs "triple tax free." For more on the ILIT, go back to Chapter 7.

Concern: You want your money to last long enough to benefit your grandchildren.

Solution: Generation-Skipping Trust (GST)

Also called a "dynasty trust", a "generation-skipping trust" (GST) is just what it sounds like: the assets put into the trust are transferred to the grandchildren rather than to the adult children. It's not necessarily about disinheriting your children. For one thing, you can set up the trust so that the children can draw the income/earnings from the trust while the grandchildren stand to inherit the balance. One big advantage to this is avoiding estate taxes. For example, let's start with a hypothetical $10 million estate, and let's say it's vulnerable to an effective 40 percent in federal and state estate taxes. If that estate passes to the children, it would be reduced to perhaps $6 million. Now suppose the children live off the earnings from the $6 million but manage to preserve the original $6 million and later pass it on to the grandchildren. Now let's suppose this time $6 million is vulnerable to a 30 percent effective estate tax. The result is that the grandchildren are receiving just $4.2 million. In such an instance, setting up a GST that gave the parents access to earnings from the trust, but kept the original funds in the trust for the grandchildren, would have accomplished pretty much the same thing but saved the grandchildren $1.8 million. These are rough numbers, but you can see how it works.

Other times, a GST is indeed about skipping a generation. Perhaps your son has remarried, and you're concerned his second wife won't necessarily pass along his wealth to the children of his first wife. If that's the case, you might not want him to ever take ownership of the assets, because once he does it becomes marital property. A GST could carve out an inheritance for them.

Note that since the minimum thresholds for estate taxes have risen so much in recent years, federal estate taxes are much more rarely a concern – at least for now.

Concern: You want your estate to reach your heirs, but you also want to take care of your spouse.

Solution: Qualified Terminable Interest Property Trust (QTIP)

Similar to a GST, a "qualified terminable interest property" (QTIP) trust can enable you to pass the earnings from assets to one person while the assets themselves will wait in trust for, say, your children, possibly decades after your death. (We told you trusts can provide flexibility!) Upon the death of the first spouse, typically what happens is that the assets of the deceased are transferred to the spouse if that spouse didn't already own them as marital property. But the QTIP (pronounced cue-tip) enables the first-to-die spouse to actually control how his or her assets are distributed after the other spouse dies. You could simply will your assets to your spouse and hope that he/she will then pass them on to your heirs. But this is not always to be expected. Suppose the spouse has children from another marriage: will they also get a piece or even most of your estate? Or suppose your spouse is terrible with money, and you wonder whether your estate will survive long enough to make it to your children. Or what if you're concerned that your spouse will remarry, and their new spouse takes marital ownership of "your" estate? The QTIP can be a perfect remedy for these concerns, because it enables you to take care of your spouse and preserve the bulk of your estate for your children. Let's say you fund a QTIP with $5 million. That $5 million would be put in a trust for your children to receive upon the death of your spouse. In the meantime, although your spouse couldn't touch the $5 million or change the trust, he/she can receive the earnings from the $5 million, which at 3 percent interest is $150,000 per year.

Concern: Your house is appreciating fast and could become a tax challenge for your heirs.

Solution: Qualified Personal Residence Trust (QPRT)

For a lot of people, giving their house to an irrevocable trust sounds rather daunting. But for some it makes financial sense. And in financial situations where our clients have second homes, such as beach homes or lake properties, we almost always talk about placing the second home in trust – specifically a "qualified personal residence trust" (QPRT).

Imagine a 50-year-old who owns a place at the Jersey Shore and plans to use the property for the rest of his life and then leave the beach home to his only son. The property today is valued at $1 million. If that property appreciates in value to $2 million and Dad's "will matures," then Junior will face the challenge of having that full $2 million included in the estate planning process and getting taxed on the full amount!

For most people, $2 million is a lot of money, even eclipsing their investable assets. It would be a shame to see it get eaten up by taxes. That brings us to the QPRT. With a QPRT, the beach home goes into a trust today for a term chosen by the settlor (in this case, Dad). The term should be shorter than his life expectancy, because the goal here is to outlive the term. At the end of the term, the ownership of the beach home will transfer to the beneficiary (in this case, his son) chosen at the outset. Now, this is a taxable event and subject to the gift tax, but the tax is based on the property's value at the date of the gift. That's very important, because the date of the gift is when the trust was established, and the property was then worth $1 million as opposed to $2 million. Keep in mind: the gift tax value is also determined by such things as the age of the grantor, the term of the retention period, the IRS Code Section 7520 interest rate established each month by the IRS and other factors. These factors can and will change from time to time. That is why it is especially important to have your estate attorney and your CPA all working on the same page with your financial advisor.

In most cases, using this strategy, the gift tax value can be discounted by 20 percent, 30 percent or even more. The real magic here is – because it's in the QPRT – the highly appreciated and growing asset (the beach home) is out of Dad's estate at a reduced gift tax value, and the appreciation of the beach home from the date of transfer is not going to be subject to tax in the future. So if Dad's $1 million property does appreciate to $2 million over the life of the QPRT, and you were dealing with a taxable estate, Dad would save about $400,000 in possible estate taxes, assuming he lives past the term of the QPRT.

When considering a QPRT, remember two key things: First, if Dad outlives the term listed in the QPRT, he does have to start "paying reasonable rent" for living at the beach home. Now, one could – and we think should – look at that as just another way to continue to transfer money from Dad's estate to the ultimate beneficiary of the QPRT: his son. Secondly, as mentioned above, Dad must outlive the term of the QPRT for the strategy to work. Why? If Dad's "will matures" within the term of the QPRT, the entire value of the beach home gets dragged back into Dad's estate as if the QPRT transfer never occurred. So all the tax savings and benefits die along with... well, you know. Once again, the team approach of having the estate attorney, CPA and financial planner all working together is crucial in this scenario.

Concern: You don't want your heir to take his IRA benefit check to the Ferrari store.

Solution: IRA Trust

Normally, with IRAs you name a beneficiary and he/she receives the money upon your death. But what if you have $3 million in your IRA and that child is 15 years old? One way to control that is to put the IRA in a trust where the child will get the money in installments well into adulthood. An IRA Trust can also be set up like a QTIP, where it can support your surviving spouse with the income it generates, but the principal assets will go to the heirs designated in the trust.

So now you have an outline of some common trusts. As you can see, estate planning can be complicated. But it's not always complicated. In fact, most of the time, it's surprisingly simple.

Trusts aren't for everybody. While we estimate that 75 percent of our clients ask if they need a trust, in the end less than half truly need one for what they are trying to accomplish. Part of the misconception and enthusiasm is surely a result of the trust marketing industry drumming up fear in people that they need a trust. Beware of the fly-by-night trust mills out there doing seminars and selling people trusts they don't really need for thousands of dollars. At best, they are selling – usually to seniors – trusts that are unnecessary. At worst, they are selling financial instruments chosen more for the sales commissions they generate than for the client's needs, and they actually leave the victim less financially secure. Whether legal or not, they are essentially scams.

How do you protect yourself? Trusts are legal documents with potentially huge consequences, and they are highly specialized for estate planning. First, your trust should always be set up by a qualified estate attorney. Second, you should also have your accountant and financial planner in the loop. As we said in Chapter 7, it's a team approach.

Time and again, we've seen trusts set up by a trust mill – or even by a qualified, well-meaning attorney – that never get funded. In other words, the client goes through the expense of setting up a trust, but if the property or funds never get transferred to the trust, the trust is completely useless after the person dies. The reason it doesn't get funded? Simply that the client never gets around to it, they forget or they never understood what needs to be done. Sometimes it involves a bullet-point list of things the client needs to do – changing the deed of the house, the name of accounts and so forth. When you have your financial advisor and accountant working on the same page, they can help handle those critical details. They can see loose ends that need tying better than the typical layman.

Another reason people are enthusiastic about trusts is a simple misconception. A lot of people think they have an estate tax problem when in reality they have an income tax problem. And although trusts can help with estate taxes, they can't eliminate income taxes. In many situations, there really is no need for a trust. Often a simple will can accomplish the same thing as a trust for a much more reasonable amount of money than what a trust would cost (often a few thousand dollars). That would be a key question for your attorney: Can I accomplish the same thing through wording in my will? Remember, while trusts can be the perfect vehicle – even an essential vehicle – not everybody needs one. Only a minority of our clients actually need a trust to accomplish what they want to accomplish.

In general, we find that people tend to overcomplicate estate planning. Either they create trusts they don't really need or they create trusts that control too much for too long after they are gone. We've been on the other side of it, where heirs are unnecessarily struggling to reach funds that are blocked by onerous trust provisions. We try to preach resisting the urge to rule from beyond the grave – and embracing flexibility.

When you get down to it, estate planning can be surprisingly simple, even for people with sizable assets. Everyone needs a will, a living will and a power of attorney. The will spells out your wishes upon your death. A living will spells out your wishes in the event you become incapacitated. A power of attorney enables someone to act on your behalf if you become incapacitated. Those are the basics to estate planning, and very often they can cover everything in terms of documents.

One other basic of estate planning is a simple detail: making sure your accounts are properly titled with the proper beneficiaries. The beauty of IRAs, Roth IRAs, 401(k)s and life insurance policies – from an estate planning perspective – is that they can pass immediately and easily to the beneficiary upon one's death. So they can be handled outside the will, and the money can be transferred directly in a manner of days. There's no lawyer to go through. No courthouse to visit. All a beneficiary needs is a certificate of death, and the money is theirs. (As we talked about in Chapter 7, the tax consequences can be severe, but at least you have the money.)

On the other hand, if the beneficiaries aren't identified properly, this inexpensive, quick and painless process can turn into something long, costly and aggravating. If no beneficiary is named in an IRA, the funds will be dispersed in accordance with the will or, in the case of no will, through the probate process. This can last 12 to 18 months and is subject to the interpretation of the will (or state law if there is no will), and it often requires significant legal fees – typically 3 percent to 5 percent of the estate's value. Naming beneficiaries doesn't cost you anything, and doing so can prevent some tremendous headaches.

Every account should have a primary beneficiary and a contingent beneficiary. For instance, if you name only your spouse as beneficiary and you and your spouse die in a car accident, that would leave no living beneficiary to receive the assets. Make sure you consult with a qualified tax advisor for the proper way to title the IRA. It should be titled as a "beneficiary IRA" account or an "inherited IRA", which will allow the beneficiary to stretch the IRA. If it's not set up properly and handled properly during the transition, it could mistakenly and immediately become a taxable event just by having it titled incorrectly. And there are no do-overs.

One more thing: Look at your estate planning documents annually. Don't just leave them in a safe deposit box for 20 years. Again, the only certainty is the randomness of life. Marriages, divorces, the death of a beneficiary, or changes in the tax laws — any of these things can change your estate plan drastically.

Some people like to say: "The perfect estate plan would be to spend your last dollar with your last breath." But in reality, if you've accumulated any wealth at all, your dollars will be spent long after your last breath. Estate planning is about seeing that those dollars are spent on or by the right people according to your wishes.

Chapter 8 Dividends

1. Most often, people can accomplish their estate planning needs using a simple will and don't require the expense of a trust.

2. Generally speaking, a trust won't help you or your heirs avoid taxes.

3. What trusts can do very effectively is provide a level of control over funds passed onto heirs.

4. One of the easiest and most important parts of estate planning is making sure your retirement accounts are properly titled with beneficiaries.

Chapter 9

In Retirement, Cash Flow is King

"Don't judge each day by the harvest you reap but by the seeds you plant."

-Robert Louis Stevenson

When the financial crisis struck in 2008 and 2009, things got a little scary. This wasn't just a rainy day. This was a 100-year flood. The downturn – now called the "The Great Recession" – was by far the deepest recession since the mid-1940s and arguably the most painful recession since the 1930s. Financial institutions were collapsing. News articles discussed the potential for bank runs. The U.S. auto and construction industries – two of the biggest industries in the U.S. – were on the ropes. Jobs were being lost by the hundreds of thousands each month.

For retirees, what made this recession particularly cancerous was how it struck all asset classes. The stock market bottomed in March 2009 at the end of a painful free-fall – nearly a 40 percent decline. There was nowhere to earn more than a shred of interest. Savings and money market accounts offered bottom-of-the-barrel returns. But at least retirees had equity in their homes, right? Nope. In much of the U.S. and around the world, home values were ravaged. It was not unheard of for a retiree to watch his or her net worth shrink by a third or more. Not just their stock portfolio, but their entire net worth – shrunk by as much as a third in just six months.

But despite this nearly unprecedented financial tumult, our clients rode out the storm without selling at market lows. How could that be? Someone was certainly selling to drive stock prices down. Why wouldn't it be our clients – retirees who didn't have youth or a job to help weather such market risk? The answer is because we showed them one very important, rarely mentioned idea: *Retirement is a cash flow game.*

We are big champions of the idea that retirement is a cash flow game. And apparently we are rare. You won't hear many financial advisors talk about retirement cash flow at all. Cash flow isn't something you plan for, they think; it's just a spigot you turn on when the money is needed. In fact, very likely, even many financial advisors reading this are puzzled right at this moment. What do we mean "cash flow is king?"

Good question. A lot of people think about saving for retirement as simply a matter of amassing a big pile of wealth. Once a man we were advising told us his only financial goal was to arrive at the end of his life with as many zeroes as possible attached to his name. And most financial advisors at least tacitly agree with that approach. They will tell their clients, if you want to live on an annual retirement spending of "X" amount, you will need 20 times "X" and you'll need to earn "Y" in investment returns so everything won't run out for "Z" number of years.

That's a snapshot of the "big pile" mentality. Frankly, creating a list of assumptions feels good. It gives you a sense of control – in a hypothetical world. The bigger X is, the less you have to worry about Y and Z. The problem is that the "big pile" isn't exactly the goal. Don't get us wrong: we think everybody should build wealth. (One of our missions in life is helping people do exactly that.) But wealth alone isn't the goal. Rather, the goals should be what wealth can bring you: financial independence, new experiences, fun, freedom and comforts. Now, running hypothetical numbers isn't in itself a bad thing. In fact, it's hard to avoid at least some of that in retirement planning. But there is a distinction between planning to have a pile and planning a successful retirement.

The reality: if any of X, Y or Z changes a little, it can drastically short-circuit the whole plan, causing anxiety and austerity in what were expected to be the golden years.

As we said, we don't believe the big pile itself is the end goal. Rather, the gauge for successful retirement planning is the quality of life and financial independence in your post-work life.

Where a lot of advisors don't follow through is in laying out a very clear income and distribution strategy. They plan for the "First Half" – accumulation during working years – but not the "Second Half."

And there's a vicious cycle at work here. Not only is the "big pile" approach incomplete. It also provides a false sense of security. That seemingly big pile of money can feel like having a dragon in your corner: nothing can touch you. After all, for most of us, the money we've accumulated entering retirement is the biggest balance we'll ever see in our lifetimes. The problem is, that pile of money also has to accomplish some things we've also never seen in our lifetimes. (When was the last time you supported yourself and a spouse for 20 or 30 years without working?)

WHY EMPHASIZE CASH FLOW?

So how can proper cash flow planning make things different? Let's start with a metaphor that might help shift you to the Second-Half mind set. Imagine, for a moment, where your water comes from. Most modern plumbing systems work something like this: A local government body draws water from a source – a river, an aquifer, a reservoir, a lake, etc. The government then treats the water and pumps it around town through a series of pipes, while households then tap into that circulation using their own pipes and plumbing systems. If you've ever turned on your faucet and water didn't come out, the first thing you thought was probably not: "Oh my goodness, the reservoir must have dried up." No, more likely, you thought something went wrong in the system that brings you the water. Maybe the city workers went on strike. Maybe you forgot to pay the bill. Maybe a trunk line failed. Maybe your husband swung a pickaxe though the pipe that feeds the house. It would be strange to think the reservoir suddenly vanished. The point is that in Second-Half financial planning, focusing on the pile of money – although everybody does it – is equally strange. Sure, you need the reservoir to be there, and being deeper is better than being shallow. But the reservoir won't do you much good if the water isn't delivered reliably. Second-Half financial planning, like plumbing, is about proper flow more than it is about the size of the reservoir.

Consider one example of how focusing on the reservoir can be short-sighted. Let's say you have $1 million in retirement savings, and the plan is to draw $30,000 a year, or 3 percent, from that. That's a reasonably conservative draw rate. Then you decide to relocate to warmer weather, and the change in housing costs $200,000. Now you're down to $800,000. Then the market tanks, and suddenly $30,000 is being drawn from what is now $500,000, and that 3 percent is now 6 percent. Your draw rate has become a burn rate, because you are burning right through your savings. Now you're nervous, and there's not much you can do about it because you're, well, retired.

PLANNING WITH CASH FLOW IN MIND

So what can be done to avoid that? Well, just as the plumbers carefully map out how the water is going to get to you, a financial planner should map out how your cash is going to flow in retirement. And the mapping method we like is the "three buckets" approach. You might recall from Chapter 1:

Bucket No. 1: Cash and liquidity – This includes your checking or savings accounts. This is the money you can withdraw from the bank immediately and the money you use for day-to-day spending.

Bucket No. 2: First-Half investments – These assets are different from bucket No. 1 in that they are positioned for some growth and income but also provide a contingency that can be accessed penalty free within a few days. For instance, these funds could be used if you need to replace the roof or buy a new car.

Bucket No. 3: Second-Half investments – These assets are specifically positioned to provide you with 100 percent of your retirement income when combined with any other income you are receiving on a monthly basis (i.e., pension and Social Security).

The underlying idea behind the buckets is to position every dollar so it works toward a goal. If you have a goal of providing your grandchildren with college money, we can set up a fourth bucket for that. Or if you want to maintain a lake house for the extended family to meet summer after summer, we can add a bucket for that. This isn't about a pile. This is about dreams being realized.

Furthermore, in building the cash flow plan, we try to reach the point where 30 to 50 percent of your retirement funds, along with Social Security and any pension income, are generating 100 percent of your retirement income. If we can achieve that, then the remaining 50 to 70 percent of your assets can be positioned for some growth for tomorrow or maybe – dare we say? – used for something fun! Now, that's a goal, but what we hope you're seeing is that once the roadmap is established for how the cash is going to flow, the emphasis shifts from the pile of money to the cash flow. With 50 to 70 percent growing untouched, the reservoir of cash becomes just like the reservoir of water. It's not on your mind. You don't look at it every day. Inevitably it will experience ups and downs, but those ups and downs have little to do with whether the water flows when you turn the spigot.

We started this chapter talking about the financial crisis and how our clients never panicked and never sold. That's because together we put a distribution system in place that gave them confidence in their cash flow first. Just like everybody else during the Great Recession, their reservoir endured a severe dry spell – the most severe in a generation. But it didn't affect their cash flow – and so really, it didn't affect them.

DESIGNING A SYSTEM THAT FLOWS WELL

So now that we understand a little more about the reason for emphasizing cash flow, let's look a little more closely at some strategies to do that. When we say cash flow is king in retirement, we specifically mean after-tax cash flow.

When we started out, Gary was a CPA from the "tax" side and Kevin was a CFP® from the "investment" side. Today, decades later, Kevin says he can't imagine doing retirement planning without a very strong understanding of the tax code. Having your tax advisor and your investment advisor on the same page is crucial. We'll say it again: Second-Half planning is a team game. And the importance of understanding taxes as they relate to investing is why every 401(k), IRA or mutual fund statement says at the bottom, in not so many words, "Please see your tax advisor." But all too often, investment advisors and tax advisors work completely independently and unaware of each other.

And the tax implications become even bigger with Second-Half investing because the amounts are usually bigger, and you're at a stage in your life where you need to start moving assets out of shelters rather than into them. But there are tax-advantaged ways of doing it. For one thing, as discussed in Chapter 6, consider converting some funds – the maximum you can convert without pushing you into a higher tax bracket – from traditional tax-deferred IRAs to tax-free Roth IRAs. Also, when you're drawing funds from a traditional IRA, do so slowly enough to minimize the ticking tax time bomb. How you withdraw the funds from investment accounts can push you into a higher tax bracket. For instance, suppose you're taking $30,000 out of your IRA each year for basic living, and then you suddenly need a new car. Taking another $30,000 out in the same year for the car can throw you into a higher tax bracket, and suddenly the $30,000 car costs a lot more than $30,000. With proper positioning and keeping enough funds in the right buckets, surprise expenses can be solved more tax efficiently. Also, to keep taxes low, as we discussed in Chapter 5, taking slow and steady disbursements from your retirement accounts can be the most tax advantaged approach. Most people, understandably, are inclined to leave funds they don't need in an IRA so those funds can continue to grow tax deferred. But the problem again is the ticking tax time bomb. When the required minimum distributions (RMDs) kick in at age 70 ½, if the IRA is big enough, the mandatory distribution could lift you into a higher tax bracket. But if you start the distributions early – say, after age 59 ½, the earliest you can typically take distributions without penalty – and you have some space left before you would reach the next tax bracket, it likely pays to take the funds out and pay the lower tax rate on those funds rather than paying a higher one later. The difference can really add up through your retirement years.

STRETCH THAT MORTGAGE IF YOU CAN

If you find yourself with a mortgage in retirement, our recommendation – almost always – is to stretch that out as long as you possibly can. Again, this goes against conventional wisdom, which is that the goal is to pay off the mortgage as soon as you can. Why do people think they need to pay off their mortgage sooner than later? Surely, some people just like to tie up loose ends. For others, there's a sense of security in it. There's probably a sense that retirees should have paid off their mortgages by now. All of these reasons stem from the First-Half mindset that seems to say: "It's debt. Therefore, it's to be paid off as soon as possible." But when you're retired, as we keep saying, cash flow is king. (Now, don't get us wrong: just because cash flow should be the primary focus doesn't mean continuing to grow your wealth isn't very important too. Growing assets is still very important. But it does take a back seat to cash flow.) And paying more than you must toward a mortgage is counterproductive to cash flow. A lot of 70 year olds will pursue a 15-year mortgage. But we say: if you can get it, go for a 30-year mortgage with a lower payment. What good does it do you to pay off your mortgage in your 80s? You would be much better served by having a smaller cash out flow, which means more flexibility in your income and spending. As we've said before, you should expect to enjoy spending in your golden years. Paying down a mortgage is really just the opposite of that. It's essentially saving. And if you die with a mortgage balance, the bank doesn't get jilted. The bank will get its money when the house is passed on to the heirs. But time and again, we encounter people trying to pay off mortgages like they are 40 year olds, not 70 year olds.

THE MINDSET

We hope that after reading this chapter and some of the preceding ones, you're starting to see that retirement is not all about having the biggest pile of money. All too often, we find people tend to "live small" because they are so focused on the pile. Because the pile is so big and abstract – not to mention, at times it can fluctuate wildly – they have real trouble ever answering the question, "Will I have enough?" But for those with the right distribution plan in place, where things are broken down into buckets, where the cash flow is managed in a tax-advantaged way and where the size of the pile is de-emphasized, they can better visualize how this is going to work out. But some are still worried the river will dry up. They are afraid to have a tall glass of water. Sometimes these folks do amass even greater sums of wealth. But they do much less in retirement. We think they miss out on some important stuff. Amassing huge amounts of money might make your kids and grandkids happy. (It'll probably make Uncle Sam happy too!) But it's not going to do you a lot of good. Or even worse, those fearful people scrimp and save, but then a lot of the money just goes to the government. The irony: all that money was supposed to provide financial independence, but without a proper distribution strategy it can do just the opposite.

Chapter 9 Dividends

1. If your retirement cash flow is well planned, your retirement happiness doesn't have to go up and down with the market.

2. A cash flow plan should be tax efficient. The "three buckets" approach enables you to deal with unforeseen expenses in a more tax-efficient manner.

3. Aggressively paying down mortgage debt is a First-Half strategy. When cash flow is king, stretching that mortgage as long as possible can make more sense.

Chapter 10

Will I Have Enough?

"I've got all the money I'll ever need, if I die by four o'clock."
— Henny Youngman

Well, if you've read this far into our book, pat yourself on the back. You've proven two things: You're serious about your Second-Half finances, and you're comfortable considering uncomfortable subjects – money, the future, death and uncertainty.

Why are these uncomfortable topics? Because what we are really talking about here is fear.

If there was one thing we could do for each one of our clients – if we could do just one thing – it wouldn't be to ensure they average a certain return on their investments. It wouldn't be to make sure they don't outlive their money. It wouldn't be to make sure they have enough left over for their heirs. Yes, we try to do all those things. But if we could only choose one thing, instead it would be: to help alleviate their financial fears.

Fear and finance go together like electricity and water – not well! And unfortunately, they go together way too often. In fact, we'd be willing to bet that in investment houses around the world "fear" is uttered many times more often than its close cousin "greed" on a daily basis. Fear is such an invasive part of finance that up to a point, it works like this: the more money one has, the more likely that person is to be fearful. Read that again. It's incredible but true. Think about it. Who's more fearful, the 20 year old just finishing college with a negative net worth, or the retiree who has $1.2 million in assets? Usually, based on our experience, it's the retiree – by a long shot. It should be the opposite. Money should make you feel more confident, not less. But still, we've lost count of the number of retirees we've encountered who were essentially living in fear. These are people without a Second-Half strategy or an income and distribution plan. And each month, they look at their balance statements fluctuating with the markets. We see so many people who live their entire retirement on an emotional yo-yo tied to the Dow Jones Industrial Average. One day the DJIA is up, and they're ready to buy a boat. The next day it's down, and they're saying, "Oh no, we can't go out to dinner." And we hear from our clients all the time, "I don't want to be thinking about this constantly." Keep in mind: we're talking about people who have money. Is all this worry nuts? Maybe a bit. But people make the mistake of mixing finances and fear.

And for folks in the Second Half of their lives, that fear can be encapsulated in four words: Will I have enough?

- Will I have enough after my spouse is gone?

- Will I have enough so my grandchildren can go to college?

- Will I have enough if I need nursing home care?

- Will I have enough to live the kind of retirement I want?

- Will I have enough to weather any financial storms?

- Will I have enough if I live to be 95... 100...110?

- Will I have enough to keep the lake house for the family?

The antidote to fear is the confidence that comes from preparation and understanding. Nothing builds confidence like being properly prepared and knowing the score. Courage, it's been said, is the opposite of fear. But fear's biggest enemy isn't courage. It's *confidence*, because confidence is based on preparation and understanding. Courage, which can come from anywhere, could disappear in a moment's notice. Confidence sticks around.

So this being the last chapter, it's time to present our call to action, if you will. You've made it this far into this book. You're ready for this simple but challenging question: Wouldn't you prefer to be confident in your Second-Half finances? Because – make no mistake – you can be.

Our recommendation is to find a financial advisor who has you and your retirement in mind. If you have a financial advisor who is calling you twice a year with a "good buy" on a stock or another investment idea, that is "First Half" stuff. Ask your financial planner for an income and distribution strategy for retirement. If they look at you quizzically, thank them for their years of service and find someone else.

12-4-2... AN APPROACH THAT WORKS

Second-Half financial planning isn't a one-shot deal. This is an ongoing process. When you're planning with a 10-, 20- or maybe 30-year time horizon, change is about the only thing you can count on. Whether it's change in the tax laws, changes in your situation or changes in the marketplace, change will happen. Because of that, we recommend that you have an ongoing relationship with your financial advisor.

We take a "12-4-2" approach with our clients, and you should expect something similar from your financial advisor.

The "12" means we check in once each month, typically by phone or email, to discuss our latest thoughts and ideas regarding your financial plan and investments and to answer your questions. Financial questions pop up all the time, and very rarely do they pop up when you are in your financial planner's office. In fact, those questions seem to have no regard for the nine-to-five workday. Rather, such questions tend to surface early in the morning or late at night – your quietest times of the day, when reaching for the phone isn't really feasible. Often they are forgotten. But if you're in the habit of having a monthly call with your advisor, the quality of dialog can improve dramatically. Instead of saying to yourself, "I've got to bring that up with my advisor," and then forgetting about it for months (which often can mean "forever"), a call is probably already arranged and is usually at most just a few weeks away. Because of that, you're more likely to remember your questions, and you're more likely to write them down, knowing the phone call is already set up. In short, monthly calls make for more proactive financial planning.

The "4" refers to four quarterly calls or meetings with your financial planner. This should be a more detailed look at the performance of your financial plan. Meeting merely annually to measure performance is too little. After all, just about every company in the world meets quarterly with its shareholders to discuss the trajectory of the business. You're the No. 1 shareholder in your retirement, and the success of that "venture" means everything to you. You should be meeting quarterly with your management team, and they should be telling you in great detail how the "business" is doing. The quarterly contact should also always address any open items in your financial plan. Again, circumstances change. Does your plan – your will, your investments, your beneficiaries, your tax strategy – need updating in any way? Changes to your plan can be critical and often shouldn't wait a whole year to be implemented.

The "2" refers to the most important piece of the 12-4-2 service combination, which is the twice-a-year, face-to-face meeting. This is the time to review in detail your overall 360-degree Second-Half financial plan and the various strategies and investments in place. In these meetings, you and your advisor should go over all the changes in your personal life that can impact your plan and consider adjustments to the plan based on those changes. With all the uncertainty and volatility out there today, at least twice a year we want to make sure we are face-to-face with our clients looking at their entire Second-Half plan to ensure we are on course and all working toward the same goal: what's important to you!

Also, we consider the 12-4-2 approach to be a minimum level of service. The lines of communication should remain open, and concerns that arise don't have to wait until a scheduled meeting to be addressed.

There is a difference – all the difference in the world, really – between promising a level of service and actually doing it. Most financial advisors out there will talk profusely about staying in touch and how they are 100 percent there for you. But we suggest you keep score.

If you're not talking regularly, seek a new financial advisor. We use the 12-4-2 approach. Other planners might have an approach that's not identical but is similar enough. The point is, this should give you an idea of what to expect from any financial advisor who's worth keeping.

THE COMPLETE PICTURE

Second-Half financial planning is about more – a lot more – than just managing your investments. Imagine a skipper at the helm of a sailboat trying to get from point A to point B. She checks the trim of her sails, she monitors the ocean current, she watches how the boat is heeling, she watches her compass heading and she watches the wind direction. Focusing only on investments would be like a captain focusing on only one element of sailing. You could focus on the trim of the sails, but if the wind changes, you and your perfectly trimmed sails could wind up on a rocky shore.

Investments are important, but they are just a piece of Second-Half financial planning. Growing and maintaining wealth involves many facets: investing, tax planning and asset protection, to name a few. And working on one facet without keeping an eye on all the others could land you on the rocks or at least slow you down. Imagine focusing on your investments and making them grow but ignoring the tax implications or forgetting to get these growing assets properly reflected in your estate plan. That approach could be disastrous.

INVESTMENT PLANNING
& RISK MANAGEMENT

WEALTH TRANSFER
& LEGACY PLANNING

RETIREMENT PLANNING

INCOME &
DISTRIBUTION PLANNING

SECOND-HALF
FINANCIAL
PLANNING

ESTATE PLANNING

SURVIVOR PROTECTION

ASSET PROTECTION

TAX PLANNING

As financial advisors, we place ourselves in the middle of this diamond. Our No. 1 guiding principle is what's important to you. Your goals and your investments are different things. Yes, the investments are often a means to achieving those goals. But they are not the same. The goal for the sailor is to get to point B, not to make the boat go faster. They might often seem to be the same thing. Doesn't going faster get you to point B sooner? Answer: only if the boat has the proper heading. That's the value of Second-Half financial planning. If you focus solely on the investments, even if you're successful, you might create a bigger pile of money. But if you ignore the other elements of wealth management, you could see a large chunk of those newfound investment earnings go to the government or to long-term care costs and not to your kids and grandkids or to whomever or whatever is important to you. That's how investment earnings can at times differ from the goal. Second-Half financial planning is centered around – we'll say it again – what's important to you. For most people, that includes not outliving their assets and protecting their spouse and heirs after they're gone.

One of the most important facets of Second-Half financial planning – and one that most people and even many financial planners ignore – is the integration of tax planning. Based on our experience, more than 90 percent of people file their tax return in a drawer and never look at it again. Most people have financial advisors who have never seen – and worse, never asked for – their tax returns. This happens mostly because the financial planners never think to ask for it or aren't qualified to do tax planning. Meanwhile, there is a total disconnect between the person who does their taxes, who likely is doing just tax preparation – not tax planning – and the financial advisor who doesn't consider tax implications, because it's uncharted territory for him. It's so important to look at all the facets together.

FLATTEN YOUR FEARS

As we said, the antidote to fear is the confidence gained from preparation and understanding. When dealing with preparation and understanding, the right financial planning team working together can help tremendously. So our challenge to you today is to chart a course to help mitigate your Second-Half financial fears. Start by asking your financial advisor for a Second-Half income and distribution strategy, so you don't have to worry about market fluctuations or whether your savings will last. Ask your estate planner, accountant and financial advisor to communicate with each other to achieve comprehensive Second-Half financial planning, so you don't have to worry about whether your investments are aligned with your goals. Start communicating with your financial advisor on a monthly basis so you can understand how your finances will hold up in a lengthy retirement. Ask your financial planners, "What are my goals?" You know the answer. Do they?

We've said a number of times that a "team approach" is best when it comes to Second-Half planning. And that's true. But you, your spouse and your heirs are the only real stakeholders in this endeavor. That might seem scary. But the answer to replacing that fear with confidence is within these pages. That's been our mission: to give you the knowledge to obtain, step by step, the confidence to enjoy your retirement. Start today. Your heirs will thank you. Your spouse will thank you. And you will have the confidence to enjoy your Second Half without financial fear.

CHAPTER 10 Dividends

1. Success in the First Half of your financial life doesn't always guarantee success in the Second Half of your financial life.

2. Does your financial advisor have a Second-Half income and distribution strategy for you?

3. You should be hearing from your financial advisor on a regular basis.

4. Second-Half financial planning is about a lot more than just your investments, and it involves a team approach.

ABOUT THE AUTHORS

Kevin D. Houser, CFP®, CES
CERTIFIED FINANCIAL PLANNER™ Professional
Certified Estate & Trust Specialist (CES)

Kevin is a senior partner and co-founder of the Houser & Plessl Wealth Management Group, LLC, located in Allentown, Pa. Kevin is a CERTIFIED FINANCIAL PLANNER™ (CFP®) and a Certified Estate & Trust Specialist (CES) concentrating on wealth protection and transfer strategies. Kevin has more than 20 years of financial planning and investment experience. His primary focus areas include estate, insurance and trust planning. Kevin graduated Magna Cum Laude from Moravian College with a degree in financial economics.

Gary T. Plessl, CFP®, CPA

CERTIFIED FINANCIAL PLANNER™ Professional
Certified Public Accountant (CPA)

Gary is a senior partner and co-founder of the Houser & Plessl Wealth Management Group, LLC, located in Allentown, Pa. Gary is a CERTIFIED FINANCIAL PLANNER™ (CFP®) and a Certified Public Accountant (CPA). Gary leads the tax practice of the Houser & Plessl Wealth Management Group and focuses on tax minimization and investment/risk planning for clients. Gary has more than 20 years of financial services industry experience in tax, financial planning and investment management. Gary holds an MBA in finance as well as an undergraduate degree in accounting from Lehigh University in Bethlehem, Pa.

Kevin D. Houser and Gary T. Plessl are registered representatives with and securities offered through LPL Financial. Member FINRA/SIPC. Houser & Plessl Wealth Management Group is unaffiliated with LPL Financial.

The opinions voiced in this material are for general information only and are not intended to provide specific advice or recommendations for any individual. The opinions expressed in this material do not necessarily reflect the views of LPL Financial. Tax law and estate law are subject to change at any time. We encourage you to consult a qualified tax planning advisor as well as an estate planning attorney in addition to your financial advisor prior to taking any action.

49981243R00074